Refresher A2

W0233969

Gaynor Ramsey

Langenscheidt

Berlin · München · Wien · Zürich · New York

English Network Refresher A2 – New Edition

Autorin:
Gaynor Ramsey, Zürich

Beratung:
Lynda Hübner, München
Carolyn Kilday-Wittmann, München
Roswitha Fenes, Bergisch-Gladbach
Vanessa Clark, Abingdon, GB

Redaktion:
Helge Sturmfels (Projektleitung)
Carola Jeschke, Haimhausen

Grafik und Layout:
Design Im Kontor – Iris Steiner, München, Gestaltungskonzept und Layout
kaltnermedia, Bobingen, Satz und Layout
Sabine Nasko, München, Umschlag

Lehrwerkskomponenten:	
Kursbuch mit Pocket Grammar A2 und Lerner-CD	50 471
Text-CD	57 771
Lehrerhandreichungen	50 472
Lehrwerksbegleitend:	
Activity Book	50 508
Pocket Reader	50 505

Acknowledgements:
The material reproduced in this book has been taken from the following sources:

Illustrations
Liili Palmer, Rockenburg: pages 86, 87, 110 – Jaqueline Urban, Berlin: page 23

Photographs
Action Press, Hamburg: pages 24, 44 (top, middle right) – Associated Press GmbH, Frankfurt a. M.: pages 66, 74 – blickwinkel/H. Schmidbauer: page 34 – Braun GmbH: page 22 (bottom) – www.barclays.co.uk: page 62 – CINETEXT, Frankfurt a. M.: pages 4 (2nd from bottom), 5 (bottom), 31 (top, middle), 71 – Corbis GmbH, Düsseldorf: pages 4 (top, middle), 9 (3: L. Clarke, 4: Frans Lanting), 11, 12 (left: LWA-Dann Tardif/zefa; right: Anna Peisl/zefa), 15 (bottom: Jim Reed), 16 (Roger Ball), 17 (background: images.com), 18 (royalty-free), 21 (Reuters), 44 (bottom right: Phil Schermeister), 50 (Lee Snider/ Photo Images), 56 (royalty-free), 67 (Patrik Giardino), 72 (Nik Wheeler), 77, 78 (right) – Corel Stock Photo Library: pages 9 (5), 60 (left) – Philip Devlin, Berlin: page 55 – picture-alliance/dpa: pages 31 (bottom), 53 (bottom) – Getty Images: pages 5 (2nd from top), 46, 53 (top) – Hong Kong Tourist Association: page 68 – iStock International Inc., Calgary: pages 17 (Roel Hoyer), 22 (top: Tomislav), 49 (bottom: Royce Richmond; top left: Selen Sergen), 61 (Michal Koziarski), 89 (Andrea Gingerich), 91 – klipsi.com: pages 4 (2nd from top), 15 (top), 78 (left) – KPA/automotorundsport, Köln: page 33 (bottom right) – Langenscheidt Archiv: pages 33 (left), 39 (A) – Bettina Lindenberg, München: pages 33 (right), 39 (C) – Manchester Evening News: pages 4 (bottom), 37 – mengerhotel.com: page 50 – Photostock medienschmiede GmbH: cover, pages 3, 8, 9 (6) – Gaynor Ramsey, Zürich: pages 27, 29 (bottom), 32, 40, 45, 49, 73, 88 – shutterstock.com: pages 5 (top), 9 (1, 2), 28, 29 (top), 33 (middle), 39 (B), 43, 44 (left, middle left), 51, 60 (middle right, right), 79 – Tages-Anzeiger, Zürich / Beat Marti: pages 5 (2nd from bottom), 65 – Tips Images: pages 90, 92 – www.uniform.net: page 38 – Visa Europe Services Inc.: page 60 (middle left) – Visum Foto GmbH: pages 10, 85 – Wales News Pictures: pages 5 (middle), 59

We should be very grateful for any information which might assist us in tracing the copyright owners of sources we have been unable to acknowledge.

www.langenscheidt.de/englishnetwork

Der Innenteil dieses Buches wurde auf chlorfrei gebleichtem Papier gedruckt.

1 2 3 4 5 * 2010 09 08 07 06

Welcome to
English Network Refresher A2

Before you start the course, we'd like to introduce you to the book
you'll be working with: *English Network Refresher A2*.

How is the book organised?
It has **ten main units**, which are made up of:
- the *Getting ready* page (e.g. p. 15). This is a homestudy page with information about the content of
  the unit, an interesting text to read and a preview task on the grammar focussed on in the lesson.
- the *classroom* pages (e.g. pp. 16 + 17). These provide the opportunity to practise and improve skills
  in the areas of grammar, functional language, vocabulary, speaking and listening, as well as reading
  and a little writing.
- the *homestudy* pages. These should be worked through after the lesson to consolidate the unit's
  structures and vocabulary. They consist of a page with the *Language study* and *Info* text (e.g. p. 18),
  exercises on the *Over to you* page (e.g. p. 19), and the *Making progress* page (e.g. p. 20) for the
  learner to record personal progress.

Three **Extra** units come after Units 3, 6 and 10 and offer practice in using language related to work
(Extra A), to travel (Extra B); and the last one (Extra C) allows learners to play with words.

Two *Test yourself* sections (pp. 81–84) provide practice in the sort of exercises which are found in the
TELC and PET exams at the A2 level.

What's on the classroom pages of the main units?
There are various recurring features on the
classroom pages:
- *Chat*, at the beginning of the lesson, provides
  an opportunity to speak about topic-related
  themes.
- *Grammar focus* explains the grammar
  elements of the unit, with a reference to the
  Language study on the next page in case more
  information is needed.
- *Vocabulary check* – a word group related to
  the topic of the unit.
- *Listening* task(s).
- *How to say it* – useful functional phrases.
- *Listen and discuss* – a free discussion task in
  which structures which have been focussed on
  can be practised in realistic situation.

What is in the Appendix?
- The *File* section (pp. 85 ff.) which contains
  the information needed to do some of the
  intercommunicative activities in the lesson.
- The *Key* (pp. 93 ff.) to all the exercises in the
  Language study, *Over to you* and the *Test
  yourself* sections of the book.
- The *Tapescript* (pp. 97 ff.) of the texts and the
  listening tasks from the homestudy section
  which are recorded on the *Learner CD*.
- The *Vocabulary* pages (pp. 103 ff.) with the
  most important vocabulary of the unit, some
  additional relevant vocabulary, a vocabulary
  task and a writing task.
- The *Functions bank* (pp. 113 ff.) where all the
  functional language used in the book is
  collected together, plus some additional
  items.

In addition there is the **Pocket Grammar** containing grammar explanations and exercises with keys.
A **Learner CD** is included in each coursebook. Also available is a **Text CD** which has all the listening
material for classroom use recorded on it.

We hope you will enjoy using *English Network Refresher A2* and wish you every success,

Gaynor Ramsey   and the Network team

Contents

'Can do' statements

Here is an overview of what you will be able to do after successfully completing this course. The stars show in which unit these aspects of language are focussed on. (Ext = Extra units)

	U 1	U 2	U 3	Ext A	U 4	U 5	U 6	Ext B	U 7	U 8	U 9	U 10	Ext C
Listening: I can													
… understand an informal conversation about a familiar topic.	★		★		★	★		★	★	★		★	
… generally identify the topic of discussion when people speak slowly and clearly.	★	★	★		★	★	★		★	★	★	★	
… understand phrases, words and expressions immediately needed.	★	★	★	★	★	★	★			★	★	★	
… understand essential information about everyday matters.	★	★	★	★	★	★	★	★	★	★	★	★	
… identify the main point of a radio programme or announcement.											★	★	
… understand a formal conversation or interview.	★					★	★						
… understand typical telephone language.				★				★					
… compare what I hear with what I already know or have read.	★				★			★			★	★	
Speaking: I can													
… take part in an informal conversation about a familiar topic.	★	★	★		★	★	★		★	★	★	★	
… express various types of numbers.	★				★						★		★
… get simple information from others about travel and other countries.	★					★	★				★		
… give advice to another person.		★		★									
… ask someone for personal information.	★	★											
… speculate about hypothetical situations.			★								★		
… ask how people feel and talk about my feelings and emotions.									★				
… make and respond to invitations.					★								
… use phone language, and make an appointment or reservation on the phone.				★				★					
… negotiate plans and ideas with others.					★	★			★			★	★
… ask and answer questions about work and free time.		★	★		★								
… take part in a simple job interview.					★								
… compare people and things.	★				★								
… say what I like/dislike and describe personal needs, wishes and ambitions.		★	★		★	★	★					★	
… make and react to suggestions.							★						

	U 1	U 2	U 3	Ext A	U 4	U 5	U 6	Ext B	U 7	U 8	U 9	U 10	Ext C
... talk about personal obligations.										★			
... describe myself, my family, other people and where I live.	★		★			★			★				
... describe my hobbies, interests, educational background and present or recent job.	★	★			★		★						
... give short, basic descriptions of present events and describe past activities and personal experiences.	★					★	★		★		★		
Reading: I can													
... understand a simple personal letter or short narratives about aspects of everyday life.		★							★	★	★		
... understand a short informative text with unknown vocabulary.	★	★	★	★	★	★	★	★	★	★	★	★	★
... identify important information in simple newspaper or magazine articles.		★	★			★	★		★	★		★	
... skim small newspaper advertisements to locate the most important pieces of information.				★									
... find the most important information in leaflets.								★					
... understand simple instructions and rules.	★	★	★	★	★	★	★	★	★	★	★	★	★
Writing: I can													
... write simple notes on something I've heard or to express my opinions.	★	★	★			★	★	★	★	★	★	★	
... write about aspects of my everyday life.			★	★	★	★	★						
... write a short letter using simple expressions for greeting, addressing.				★					★	★			
... describe an event in simple sentences.								★		★	★		
... write a list or set of questions.				★		★							★
... fill in a simple questionnaire.	★												
... write a personal diary about my learning experiences.	★	★	★	★	★	★	★	★	★	★	★	★	★
Strategies: I can													
... ask for help if I don't understand.	★					★							
... deal with unknown vocabulary in texts and can use a dictionary effectively.			★						★				
... ask for repetition.	★												
... ask for confirmation.												★	
... use various strategies to help me make progress.			★				★			★	★	★	

Working with ...

... English Network Refresher A2

Well done! You have chosen exactly the right course to help you to reactivate your English. The units in your book have three phases: **before**, **during** and **after** the lesson. Read on to find out how you can get the most out of this course.

Before the lesson ...

look at the *Getting ready* page (e.g. p. 15). There's a text for you to read, and you can listen to it, too. This text and the question that follows it, prepare you for the topic of the lesson. There's also a short task in the *Preview* box – this prepares you for the grammar content of the lesson. If you think you need a bit of help with this, look at the page in the *Pocket Grammar* that you are referred to. Now you're ready for the lesson!

During the lesson ...

you have the opportunity to speak a lot – in pairs and in groups. Everybody is there to learn – so don't be shy, and don't worry too much about making a mistake. You'll soon see that speaking a lot helps you to reactivate your English and to correct your mistakes. The most important thing is to take part actively in the lesson. The topics in the units will certainly interest you.

After the lesson ...

you'll find some follow-up work that you can do before the next lesson. The *Language study* section (e.g. p. 18) gives you more information about the grammar. And the *Info* section on the same page gives you some interesting background information to read about and listen to. The *Over to you* page (e.g. p. 19) is a homework page with exercises. You can check your answers in the key and give yourself a score.

After that you can write your score on the *Making progress* page (e.g. p. 20) and also assess how confident you feel about the unit. If you need more help, you can go the *Pocket Grammar*, the *Vocabulary* page or the *Functions bank*. You can also write a few sentences about the last lesson in your *Personal diary* and discover strategies that will help you to learn in *Tips for learners*.

NB

After Units 5 and 10, there's a test you can do, *Test yourself* (pp. 81 ff.). The exercises are modelled on the types of exercises in *The European Language Certificate* (TELC) A2, so you can see what the level of the examination is like.

Now that you've got your *Refresher A2* book, your *Learner CD* and your *Pocket Grammar* – you're ready to start, so ...

enjoy your course!

Symbols:

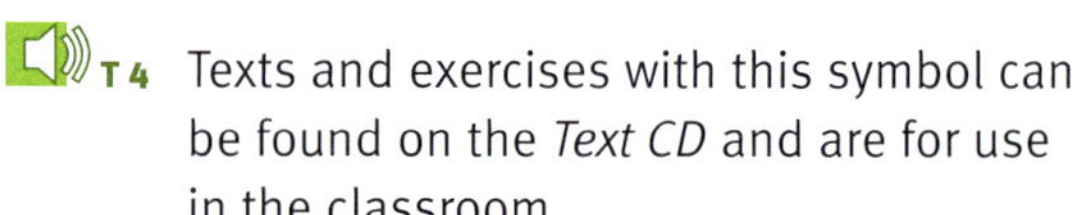 **T 4**   Texts and exercises with this symbol can be found on the *Text CD* and are for use in the classroom.

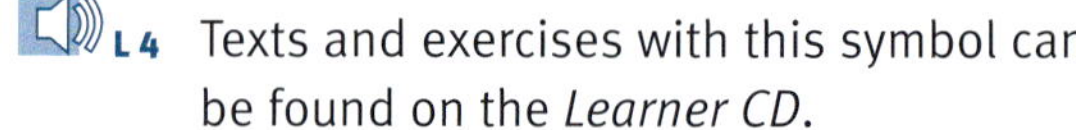 **L 4**   Texts and exercises with this symbol can be found on the *Learner CD*.

🔑   This symbol gives the page where you can find the key to homestudy exercises.

✏   This symbol refers to the writing task on the *Vocabulary* page.

www   This symbol refers to Internet tasks. The links to these tasks can be found on the website www.englishnetworklink.com.

TYS   This refers to the self-correctible test page.

PG   This refers to a page in the accompanying booklet, *Pocket Grammar*.

English around the world

English is spoken in a lot of different countries all around the world. More and more young children are learning English as their first foreign language at primary school. And it's used as the language of communication by millions of speakers of other languages. People just like you!

In which English-speaking countries do you think these photos were taken?
Have you been to any of these countries?
Do you know anybody who lives in any of these countries?
What other languages are spoken in these countries?

🔊 **L 2**

Preview

Which of these sentences tell you that the children are in class now?

☐ The children practise their English in class.
☐ The children are practising their English in class.

 page 93

1 Learning English

1 Chat

Talk to one other person in your class for five minutes. Find out some interesting things about him or her. You can decide what you want to ask about … home, job, family, holidays, favourite restaurant, etc.

Tell your class one interesting thing that you found out about your partner.

2 Using English

This task is about
- the experience of learning English that the people in your class have had
- the opportunities that people have to use their English
- what *you* want to improve and what your needs are

🔊 T 2 A man called Konrad is going to start an English class next week. His teacher wants to know more about his English.

Work with a partner.

Look at page 85.

3 Vocabulary check: Numbers

You probably said some numbers in your conversation with 'the teacher'.
Practise saying the following numbers with a partner:

1 – 20   then   30   41   52   63   74   85   96   100   107   110   1,000   9,999

Your teacher is going to say some numbers between 1 and 9,999. Write down the numbers that you hear.

4 The questions you asked

These are the words that you wrote down in exercise 2.

when   does   where   how long   do   are   why   is   what

Underline the words that you can use to ask questions about both the present **and** the past.
Circle the words that you can use to ask about the present **but not** the past.

5 Grammar focus: Present simple and present progressive ▶ LS, page 12

Our English teacher is in the office. She teaches three evenings a week at this school. But she isn't teaching now – she's talking to a new student called Konrad. She always asks new students a few questions before their first lesson.

Which verbs are about things the teacher does again and again? ☐ blue ☐ green
Which verbs are about things that are happening now? ☐ blue ☐ green

5a Things in common

Work with a partner. Write down two things that you are both doing now, e.g. *We're practising our English.*

Now find out two things that you both do. Ask *Do you …?* Write those things down, e.g. *We both drink coffee in the morning.*

Find out two things that are different. Write those things down, e.g. *(Paul) always leaves home before 7 o'clock, but I never leave home before 8.*

5b What's true?

Konrad is looking out of the window. He can see a man playing golf. Look at the photo of the man. Decide if these statements are true (T), false (F) or if it's impossible for you to say (?).

1 He's wearing a hat.
2 He plays golf every weekend.
3 He's playing golf with a woman.
4 He always plays golf with this woman.
5 He works in a book shop.
6 He's selling English books.
7 He plays golf.
8 He always wears a hat when he's on the golf course.

6 How to say it: What to say if you don't understand

Here are some sentences that you can use if you don't understand what someone says to you. Complete the sentences with these verbs: *know, mean, repeat, say, speak, understand.* Use each verb once.

I'm sorry, could you .... more slowly, please?

I'm sorry, I didn't .... you – could you .... that again, please?

Could you please .... that for me?

Sorry – I don't .... what you ....

Tick (✔) the sentence you like best. Try to use it in your discussion in exercise 7.

 T4 **Listen and discuss**

Listen to what some English teachers say about their classes in other countries. What did their students find difficult about learning English?

Which of these things are difficult for you, too?

Now go on to talk about your past experiences of learning English, or any other language.

Language study

Present simple

1 Die einfache Gegenwart beschreibt gewohnheitsmäßige, sich wiederholende Handlungen.
2 Sie wird auch in Aussagen verwendet, die allgemein gültig sind.

Write the correct forms of these verbs: a) *work*, b) *live*, c) *get*.

a) She .... three days a week – she .... on Mondays or Tuesdays.

b) .... they .... near here? – No, they .... , they .... miles away.

c) It .... light very early in Sweden in the summer.

Bitte beachten Sie: He/She/It – das 's' muss mit. In der dritten Person Einzahl wird an das Ende des Verbs ein 's' angehängt und aus *do / don't* wird *does / doesn't*.

Present progressive

1 Die Verlaufsform der Gegenwart wird verwendet, um über Dinge zu sprechen, die im Moment geschehen.
2 Sie wird ebenfalls benutzt, wenn etwas in einem Zeitraum geschieht, der noch nicht abgeschlossen ist, z.B. *today, this week*.

Write the correct forms of these verbs: d) *do*, e) *make*.

d) What .... the children .... ? They .... their English homework upstairs.

e) They .... good progress with their English in their new class.

! Den Unterschied im Gebrauch der Verlaufsform der Gegenwart und der einfachen Form der Gegenwart können Sie an folgendem Satz gut erkennen:

She usually goes to work on foot, but today she's going by bus.

page 93

info

Learning languages in the UK   The level of foreign language skills in other European countries is higher than in the UK. In a survey of nearly 16,000 people in different countries, more than half said that they could speak one other European language. About a quarter said that they could speak two other languages. But in the UK, over 65% of the people said that they did not speak any other language at all! The government wants this to change. They want every primary school to offer a foreign language to every child. At the moment there are generations of people who did not have the opportunity to learn a language at primary school. Some of them try to learn a language as adults – particularly Spanish, as Spain is the most popular European holiday and retirement destination for the British.

L 3

1 Grammar: Present simple and present progressive

Cross out the verb that is **not** correct.

My neighbours all (1) *speak / are speaking* a bit of English. Their son (2) *does / is doing* an English course on the Internet. He (3) *doesn't use / isn't using* English in his job, but he (4) *goes out / is going out* with an American at the moment and they (5) *speak / are speaking* English together. His parents (6) *brush up / are brushing up* their English in an evening class.

Write the first words in these questions, and give the short answers, e.g. *Are your neighbours nice? – Yes, they are.*

7 .... the neighbours all speak some English? – (8) ....

9 .... their son learning English at school? – (10) ....

11 .... their son speak English at work? – (12) ....

13 .... their son speak English with his girlfriend? – (14) ....

15 .... you and his parents learning English together? – (16) ....

> **1** point for each correct answer
> My score: **16**

2 Vocabulary: Question words

Which question words do you think started the questions that give the answers a)–h)?

1 how long   a) In a bookshop.
2 how many   b) Because I'm hungry.
3 when   c) That man? He's my boss.
4 where   d) Oh … three or four.
5 which   e) On Monday evenings.
6 who   f) Well, it isn't mine.
7 whose   g) About half an hour.
8 why   h) I like the blue one best.

> **1** point for each correct answer
> My score: **8**

3 L4 Pronunciation

Listen and circle the numbers you hear.

1) 13 / 30   3) 12 / 20   5) 89 / 98
2) 16 / 60   4) 18 / 80   6) 108 / 180

L5 Now listen and repeat the numbers.

> **1** point for each correct answer
> My score: **6**

4 L6 Listening

Konrad's English teacher is talking to another teacher after the first lesson. Listen and choose the correct information.

1 This class is ☐ *bigger than* ☐ *the same size as* ☐ *smaller than* her last class.

2 The people in the class are ☐ *all teenagers* ☐ *of mixed ages* ☐ *all senior citizens.*

3 Most of the learners last had an English lesson ☐ *last year* ☐ *years ago.*

4 Most of the learners ☐ *use* ☐ *don't use* English at work.

5 ☐ *None* ☐ *Most* ☐ *All* of the learners are willing to work a lot and do homework.

> **1** point for each correct answer
> My score: **5**

5 How to say it: Asking for help with spoken language

Match the two parts of these sentences.

1 Sorry, I don't know   ☐ a) a little English!
2 Could you repeat   ☐ b) mean exactly?
3 What does …   ☐ c) what you mean.
4 Do you think you could speak   ☐ d) that, please?
5 I only understand   ☐ e) more slowly, please?

Now match the sentences to these situations.

☐ You want to hear what the person said again.
☐ The other person can speak better than you.
☐ You don't understand a word that was used.
☐ You don't understand the general message.
☐ The other person is speaking too fast for you.

> **1** point for each correct answer
> My score: **5**

Over to you
My total score: [ ] **40**

40–36 = Excellent **35–31** = Very good **30–26** = Good
25–21 = Okay **20 or below** = You need a bit more practice.
Look at the **Help** suggestions in the **Checkpoint**.

CHECKPOINT

How confident do you feel about what you've learnt and practised? Tick the appropriate boxes.

Help

Grammar focus: Present simple and
present progressive
*She usually goes to work on foot, but today
she's going by bus.*
▶ Pocket Grammar,
   pages (6, 7) **11**

Vocabulary: Numbers, question words
▶ Vocabulary, page 103

How to say it: What to say if you don't understand
▶ Functions bank, page 113

Personal diary **You and language**

Answer these questions. Write the answers in your language, if you like.

What is your mother tongue?

When and where did you learn English
before you came to this course?

What other languages do you know?

Which is your 'best' foreign language?

What is your motivation for taking this course?

What do you want to improve most?

What do you find difficult in English?

What do you find easy in English?

Tips for learners **Getting the most out of this course**

In every unit in this book, you'll find some tips on how you can learn better. But here, in Unit 1,
it's up to you to decide. What will you try to do during this course?

I want to get as much as possible out of this course, so I'll try to …

☐ *come to every lesson.*
☐ *do the homework every week.*
☐ *read something in English between lessons.*
☐ *talk to someone in English as often as possible.*
☐ *listen to something in English every week.*

☐ ....

☐ ....

Before you go on to Unit 2, try to find time to do the ***Getting ready*** page.    

- talk about the jobs that you and other people do
- focus on speaking about activities that started in the past and are still continuing (*I work ..., I have been working ...*)
- practise asking for and giving advice
- review vocabulary about the weather and about jobs

Mike Theiss at work

A risky moment when high winds nearly blew Mike away during a hurricane in 2005.

Adrenalin at work

Mike Theiss has been watching weather since he was six years old. As a young boy he often sat on the veranda of his family's house in Florida and watched thunderstorms. He loved watching the lightning and listening to the thunder.

Now he is a hurricane chaser and storm photographer. He's been doing this job for fifteen years. When a hurricane is on its way, Mike does exactly the opposite to what other people do. Most people in the area pack some personal things, make their homes as secure as possible and leave town. Mike Theiss packs his photography equipment and drives towards the hurricane. The challenge is to get as close to the eye of the hurricane as possible and take dramatic photos. This is exciting work but it can also be dangerous. 🔊 **L 7**

What other jobs do you think are exciting but also dangerous at times?

Present perfect progressive ▶ PG, page 10

*Mike Theiss **has been watching** weather since he was six years old.*

Which one of these sentences is true?

- ☐ Mike was interested in weather as a child but isn't interested now.
- ☐ Mike wasn't interested in weather at all when he was a teenager.
- ☐ Mike was interested in weather when he was six, and he's still interested now.

🔑 **page 93**

2 At work

1 Chat

Which jobs can you think of that are: a) exciting, b) dangerous, c) boring, d) stressful?

2 Your work situation

Work with a partner. Look at the words and expressions below. Make sure that you know what they mean.

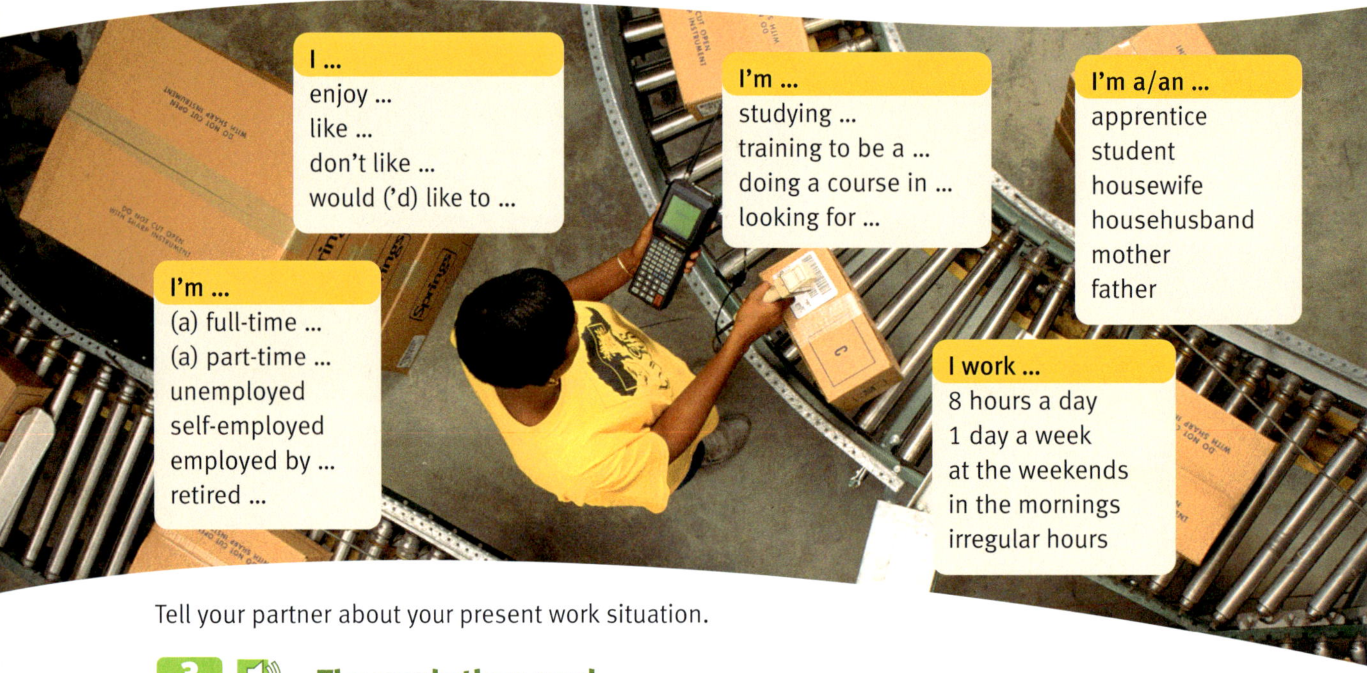

Tell your partner about your present work situation.

3 T5 The words they used

You're going to hear two people talking about work. The woman uses two words or expressions from each box above. Underline them.

Work in groups of four. What did the woman say using the words and expressions that you underlined? Are these things true for you, too? Tell the others in your group.

4 T6 How to say it: Giving advice

Listen to a later part of Rob and Kate's conversation. Complete Rob's sentences:

I think you should ....

Why don't you ....?

If I were you, I'd ....

Now you can give each other some advice. **Partner A**, look at page 89. **Partner B**, look at page 91.

5 Grammar focus: Present simple and present perfect progressive ► LS, page 18

Mike Theiss **works** as a photographer, he **takes** photographs of extreme weather, so he **doesn't spend** very much time indoors. He**'s been watching** weather since he was six. How long **has** he **been working** as a photographer? He**'s been doing** that for about fifteen years.

Which verbs tell you *only* about Mike's present working life? ☐ blue ☐ green
Which verbs tell you about Mike's present and past working life? ☐ blue ☐ green

Read this with a partner:
My neighbour is my best friend from secondary school days. She's got a job at British Airways. She started this job three years ago. Before that, she worked in the bank with me for three years.

Now choose the correct sentences.

1 ☐ She works for an airline.
☐ She works for a bank.
2 ☐ She used to work for an airline.
☐ She used to work for a bank.
3 ☐ She has been working for an airline for three years.
☐ She has been working for a bank for three years.

Complete sentence a) **or** b) about yourself and then read it to a partner.

a) I work for .... I ....

there for *(length of time)* ....

b) I live in .... I ....

there for *(length of time)* ....

Work with a partner. Find out three things about him/her, e.g. *He/She sings in a gospel choir.* Talk about home, job, learning, sport, hobby, etc.

Ask your partner questions beginning with *How long …,* e.g. *How long have you been singing in the gospel choir?* Make a note of the answers.

Work in groups of four. Tell the others about your partner. If you made a sentence with *since*, ask someone else to change it into a sentence with *for*, and vice versa, e.g. *He/She has been singing in the gospel choir **for** ten years / **since** (+ year).*

Remember

since he was six	since = seit
for about fifteen years	for = seit

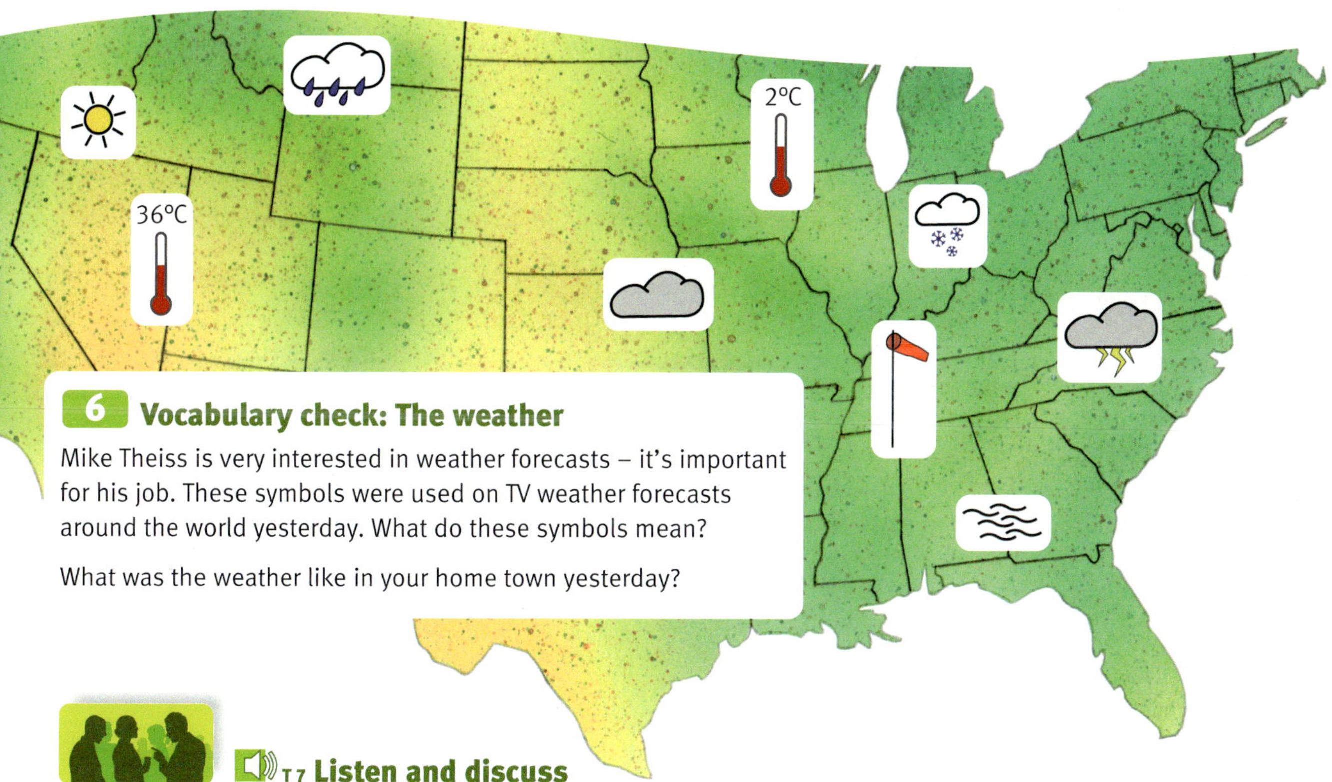

6 Vocabulary check: The weather

Mike Theiss is very interested in weather forecasts – it's important for his job. These symbols were used on TV weather forecasts around the world yesterday. What do these symbols mean?

What was the weather like in your home town yesterday?

T 7 Listen and discuss

Rob and Kate, who you listened to before, are now talking about how the world of work is constantly changing. What changes do they mention?

Computers are used in many job situations today. What do you like or dislike about computers?

Now go on to talk about a job you'd love or hate to have.

Language study

Present simple

1 Die einfache Gegenwart wird benutzt für gewohnheitsmäßige, sich wiederholende Handlungen.
2 Sie wird auch in Aussagen verwendet, die allgemein gültig sind.
3 Einige Verben (z.B. *like, hate, know, understand*) beschreiben keine Handlungen. Deshalb werden sie in den einfachen Zeiten und nicht in der Verlaufsform verwendet.

Match these sentences to explanations 1–3 above:

☐ a) Doctors and nurses work very hard.
☐ b) She goes to work by train.
☐ c) I know her boss very well.

Bitte beachten Sie: He/She/It – das 's' muss mit. In der dritten Person Einzahl wird an das Ende des Verbs ein 's' angehängt und aus *do / don't* wird *does / doesn't*.

Present perfect progressive

Die Verlaufsform der vollendeten Gegenwart wird für Aktivitäten verwendet, die in der Vergangenheit begonnen wurden und bis in die Gegenwart andauern.

Complete these questions, and answer them:

d) They live in a very modern flat. How long .... they .... there?

They .... there for six months.

e) She works in a bookshop. How long .... she .... there?

She .... there since she was eighteen.

! Den Unterschied im Gebrauch der Verlaufsform der vollendeten Gegenwart und der einfachen Form der Gegenwart können Sie an folgendem Satz gut erkennen:

*She **works** for an airline, but she**'s been looking** for a new job since January.*   🔑 **page 93**

info

Finding a job In the UK in the past, people without a job had to go to one place (a job centre) to try to find a job, and to another place (a social security office) to claim financial support (called unemployment benefit) from the government. These are now being combined into an integrated service called **Jobcentre Plus**. People can find out about jobs and retraining at a Jobcentre Plus office or from Jobcentre's Internet site. People can also get advice by calling Jobcentre's phone service, **Jobseeker Direct**. There are, of course, lots of other ways of finding a job – ads in the newspaper, agencies, friends and so on.

🔊 L 8

1 Grammar: Present simple and present perfect progressive

Write the missing words in these questions.

1 How often .... Mike Theiss see hurricanes?

2 How long .... he ....
(take) .... photographs of weather?

3 How long .... the magazines
.... (buy) .... his photos?

4 How much .... the magazines pay for his photos?

Write *since* or *for* before each of these words or expressions.
She has been doing that …

5 .... a long time.

6 .... half an hour.

7 .... ten o'clock.

8 .... a year.

9 .... she was born.

10 .... most of her life.

11 .... ten minutes.

12 .... her last birthday.

1 point for each correct word — My score: **16**

2 Pronunciation

Underline the stressed syllable in these words, like this: *syllable*

1 photographer – photograph

2 electrician – electricity

3 adviser – advice

4 politician – politics

5 policeman – police

6 musician – music

L 9 Listen and check your answers.

1 point for each correct pair — My score: **6**

3 L 10 Vocabulary: Employment and unemployment

Listen to the definitions and write the words.

1 ....   4 ....

2 ....   5 ....

3 ....   6 ....

1 point for each correct answer — My score: **6**

4 L 11 Listening

You're going to hear short parts of four different job interviews. Which job is each interview for?
Write the numbers 1–4.

☐ a teacher   ☐ a nurse
☐ a circus clown   ☐ a taxi driver
☐ a cook   ☐ a mountain guide

1 point for each correct answer — My score: **4**

5 How to say it: Giving advice and reacting to it

Give some advice to a friend. Write these words in the right order.

1 were – I – buy – one – If – that – I'd – you,

....

2 buy – that – Why – one? – you – don't

....

3 should – that – I – one – think – you – buy

....

4 better – buy – It – be – that – to – might – one

....

....

Here are four reactions to your advice. Number them 1–4 from the most positive (1) to the most negative (4).

☐ You must be joking!
☐ Yes, that's a good idea.
☐ Well … I need to think about it for a while.
☐ Yes, you may be right.

1 point for each correct answer — My score: **8**

🔑 p. 93

✏ p. 104

▶ WWW

Over to you
My total score: [ ] **40**

40–36 = Excellent   **35–31** = Very good   **30–26** = Good
25–21 = Okay   **20** or below = You need a bit more practice.
Look at the **Help** suggestions in the **Checkpoint**.

CHECKPOINT

How confident do you feel about what you've learnt and practised? Tick the appropriate boxes.

				Help
Grammar focus: Present simple and present perfect progressive *She* works *for an airline, but she's been looking for a new job since January.*	☐	☐	☐	► Pocket Grammar, pages (6, 10) **12**
Vocabulary: The weather, jobs	☐	☐	☐	► Vocabulary, page 104
How to say it: Giving advice	☐	☐	☐	► Functions bank, page 113

Personal diary Write about your last lesson.

In Unit 2, we looked at work and jobs. We talked about jobs that are dangerous …

Tips for learners Two ways of listening

In this unit you did two very different kinds of listening.

Listening for detail (exercise 3): With this kind of listening you want to hear some specific words or information. You wait for this information only, and you don't need to listen to all the other things that the people say – because they aren't relevant.

Listening for general understanding (Listen and discuss): Here you tried to understand the opinions the two people had and the comments they made. With this sort of listening you shouldn't worry if you don't understand every word. If you stop to think about individual words, you will miss part of what the people are saying. If you understand the general message, then that's fine.

Before you go on to Unit 3, try to find time to do the ***Getting ready*** page.

- talk about avoiding doing things that you don't like doing
- focus on hypothetical situations in the present *(If I won ..., I would buy ...)*
- practise talking about what you like and don't like doing
- review vocabulary about your home and what's in it

Let Wakamaru take over

We would like to introduce you to your new house-sitter, secretary and companion: Mitsubishi's robot, Wakamaru. The robot is about one metre tall, weighs less than 30 kilos, moves around on wheels and runs on batteries that it recharges by itself. The Japanese company says, "This is the start of an era in which humans and robots can co-exist."

Wakamaru could be a very useful helper to have around. He (or should it be she or even it?) doesn't need feeding, doesn't make a mess in the house and, best of all, doesn't disagree with you. Wakamaru just does what you want it to do.

But what would you like a robot to do for you? If you had a robot, would you ask it to clean your carpet or your windows? Or would you ask it to do the gardening? Can robots actually do these jobs? Perhaps you wouldn't buy a robot at all, even if you had enough money. Perhaps you would prefer to have a human house-keeper or a butler ... or both!  L 12

Would you prefer to have a robot to help you with your household chores, or a person?

Second conditional ▶ PG, page 30

A journalist said: *Even if I **had** enough money, I **wouldn't buy** a robot.*

Are these sentences true (T) or false (F)?

- [ ] He has enough money to buy a robot.
- [ ] He would like to have a robot but doesn't have enough money.
- [ ] He doesn't want to have a robot at all.

page 93

1   Chat

Which everyday chores would you like a robot or another person to do for you? Find out what the class favourite is.

2   Vocabulary check: Your home

Write down the words for all of the rooms in your flat or house, including places like the cellar and the garage … which aren't *really* rooms. Compare lists with a partner.

Now talk to your partner about the things you've got in your home. Tell him/her where these things are: *television, wardrobe, washing machine, sofa, bookshelf, mirror, telephone, shower, radio, vacuum cleaner* and *fridge*.

Now think about your kitchen. Make a list of all the kitchen appliances that you've got (big ones, e.g. a fridge, and small ones, e.g. a coffee machine), including the ones in the cupboard that you never use!

3   T8 Domestic chores

Listen to a man and a woman talking about domestic chores.

Do they:

like doing them (✔)?
dislike doing them (✗)?
not do them at all (–)?

Which of these household chores are traditionally 'men's jobs' and which are 'women's jobs'?

Write the symbols in the table.

	the woman	the man
cooking		
shopping for food		
emptying the dishwasher		
taking the rubbish out		
ironing		
working in the garden		
cleaning the windows		
cleaning the car		

4   How to say it: Likes and dislikes

Complete these sentences about domestic chores:

1 I like ....

2 I don't like ....

3 I'm not very keen on ....

4 I hate ....

Compare sentences with a partner. Did you choose the same thing for any of the sentences?

Remember

Like, hate, (not) keen on, enjoy, dislike, can't stand + -ing form of the verb,
e.g. *I really enjoy **cooking**.*

5   Grammar focus: Second conditional ▶ LS, page 24

He **would be able to employ** a gardener **if** he **were** richer.
He **wouldn't have to work** in the garden **if** he **had** a gardener.
But even **if** he **were** very rich, he **wouldn't buy** a robot.

Which would he like to have? ☐ a gardener ☐ a robot

Would you **buy** a robot **if** you **had** enough money?

Work in groups of four. Write four questions with *What (Where / How) would you do (say / feel / go / buy,* etc.) *if ... ?* Choose from these situations: *win the lottery, meet (name of a famous person), see an accident, find a stray dog, lose your house keys, win a holiday,* etc.

Each person should now take one of the questions and ask as many people as possible from other groups in five minutes. Make a note of the answers.

Go back to your group and report, like this: *Two people in our class would buy a big television if they won the lottery. One person would buy a new car.*

5b **Could he improve his life?**

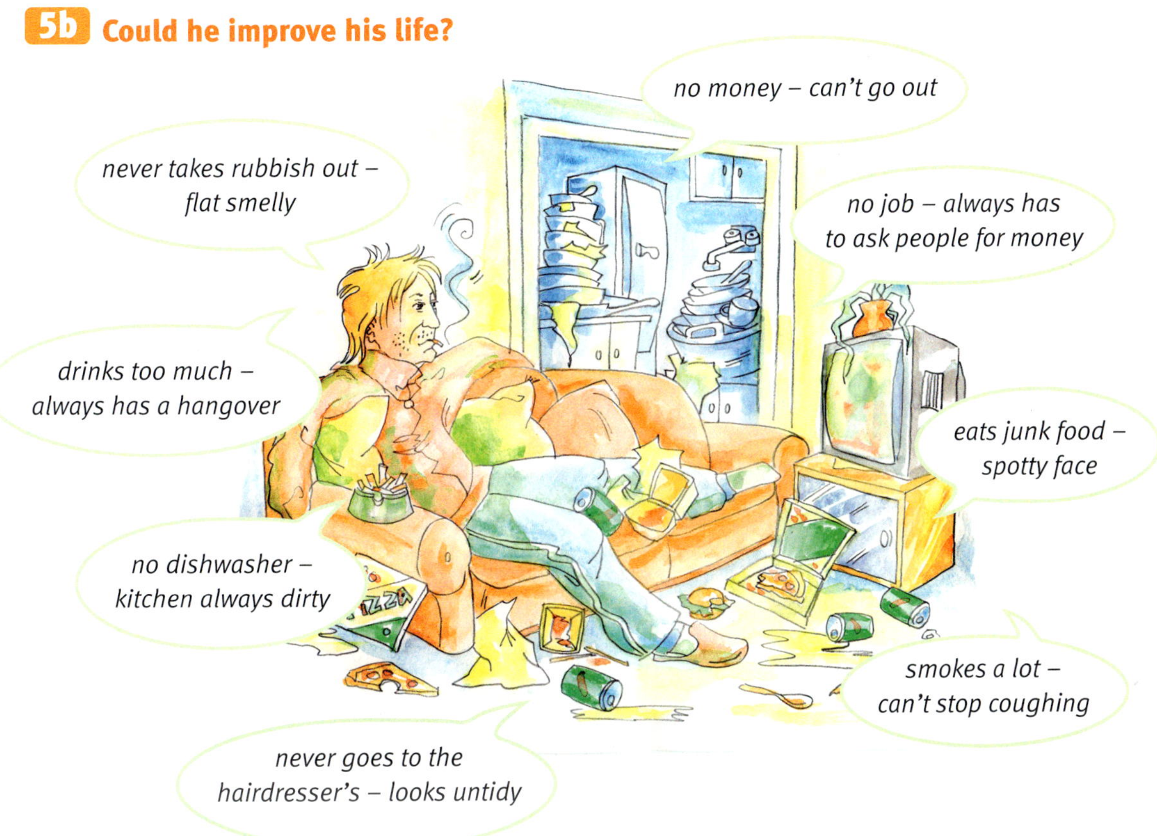

Work in small groups. What do you think are the four most urgent things for this young man to change?

Join another group and tell them your decisions about the young man, e.g. *(no alarm clock – wakes up late) If he had an alarm clock, he wouldn't wake up late.*

Go back to your original group. Make a chain story about the young man like this: *If he had an alarm clock, he wouldn't wake up late. And if he didn't wake up so late, perhaps he would be able to get up early and go out to buy a newspaper. Then perhaps he would find a job. If he ...*

T9 Listen and discuss

Colin and Claire, who you listened to before, are now talking about how domestic chores have changed since they were children. What changes do they mention?

Which of your domestic appliances would you most hate to be without? Why?

Now go on to talk about the things you like or don't like about your home and the things in it.

Language study

Second conditional

1 *If*-Sätze vom Typ 2 beschreiben eine Situation, die als solche nicht existiert, die aber vorstellbar ist.

2 Sie werden im *if*-Satz mit der Vergangenheit und im Hauptsatz mit *would* + Infinitiv gebildet.

3 Verb *be*: Es ist stilistisch besser, *were* (anstelle von *was*) bei allen Personen zu verwenden.

4 Das Wort *would* wird nur in Aussagesätzen zu *'d* abgekürzt, nicht aber in verneinten Sätzen, Fragesätzen oder in Kurzantworten.

Read these sentences and answer the questions below.
Even if he had enough money, he wouldn't buy a robot. He'd employ a gardener if he were richer. He'd feel a lot better if he didn't have to work so hard.

1 Would he like to have a robot?	a) ☐ Yes, he would.	b) ☐ No, he wouldn't.
2 Would he like to have a gardener?	a) ☐ Yes, he would.	b) ☐ No, he wouldn't.
3 Does he have enough money to employ a gardener?	a) ☐ Yes, he does.	b) ☐ No, he doesn't.
4 Does he work hard?	a) ☐ Yes, he does.	b) ☐ No, he doesn't.
5 Does he feel 100 % fit?	a) ☐ Yes, he does.	b) ☐ No, he doesn't.
6 Would he feel better if he worked less?	a) ☐ Yes, he would.	b) ☐ No, he wouldn't.

! Hier ein Hinweis zur Zeichensetzung:

If the *if* clause comes first, it is followed by a comma.
There's no comma if the *if* clause comes second.

What **would** you **buy if** you suddenly **became** very rich?

If I ...., I .... page 93

info

Robots in use today The word 'robot' was first used in 1920 in a play by the Czech writer, Karel Capek. The story was simple – a man makes a robot and then the robot kills the man! In more recent films, a lot of robots have become less aggressive towards their creators. In real life, robots are no longer just fantasy – we have been able to see them at work in car manufacturing for years. But they can also take on jobs such as cutting your grass or cleaning your floor.
Some of the most dramatic uses of robots have been seen in dangerous situations. Quite often, robots are sent into buildings or other areas to see if they can find a bomb or other dangerous material, such as chemicals. In this way, robots can save lives. The robot shown here is examining the cars for bombs or other explosives. Police in Florida, USA, wanted to question the people in the cars about their possible involvement in terrorist activities.

L 13

1 Grammar: Second conditional

Cross out the words in *italics* that are **not** correct.

1 If *she would have / she had* a lot of money, *she'd be able to go / she went* on holiday.
2 Who *will you ask / would you ask* if *you had to / you would want* to have some information about robots?
3 If *I didn't live / I don't live* near here, *I can't / I wouldn't be able to* go to this English course.
4 Even *if he had / he has* a job, *he will never have / he would never have* any money.

Write the correct form of the verbs in these sentences.

5 If he *(be)* .... the boss, I *(not work)* .... there.

6 They *(can live)* .... in America if she *(get)* .... that job.

7 I *(not go)* .... to the English class if I *(not enjoy)* .... it.

> **1** point for each correct answer My score: **14**

2 How to say it: Likes and dislikes

Number these expressions from the most positive (1) to the most negative (8).

- [ ] **I love** walking with my dog.
- [ ] **I hate** travelling in the rush hour.
- [ ] **I enjoy** relaxing on my balcony.
- [ ] **I'm not very keen on** gardening.
- [ ] **I quite like** cooking.
- [ ] **I don't mind** living in an old flat.
- [ ] **I can't stand** cleaning my windows.
- [ ] **I don't really like** shopping in big shopping centres.

> **1** point for each correct answer My score: **8**

3 L 14 Listening

First check your answers in exercise 2. Now listen to the conversation between Colin and Claire that you heard in the lesson. Listen to the expressions they use to say what they like and don't like doing. Match the expressions in exercise 2 to things they speak about.

- [ ] a) ... 'creating' in the kitchen.
- [ ] b) ... walking around supermarkets.
- [ ] c) ... cooking.
- [ ] d) ... emptying the dishwasher.
- [ ] e) ... taking the rubbish out.
- [ ] f) ... ironing.
- [ ] g) ... cleaning the bathroom.
- [ ] h) ... cleaning cars.

> **1** point for each correct answer My score: **8**

4 Vocabulary: Rooms at home

Where do people usually do these things? Most people ...

1 ... cook in the ....
2 ... sleep in the ....
3 ... take a shower in the ....
4 ... keep their wine in the ....
5 ... watch TV in the ....

> **1** point for each correct answer My score: **5**

5 Pronunciation

Underline the word in which the letters in **bold** sound different.

1 ma**ch**ine   re**ch**arge   **ch**ore
2 cou**gh**   wei**gh**   enou**gh**
3 ar**ou**nd   h**ou**se   c**ou**gh
4 cl**ea**n   **ea**sier   unpl**ea**sant
5 **c**ellar   **c**offee   **c**upboard

L 15 Listen and check your answers.

> **1** point for each correct answer My score: **5**

p. 93

p. 105

WWW

<table>
<tr><td>Over to you
My total score: [ ] 40</td><td>40–36 = Excellent   35–31 = Very good   30–26 = Good
25–21 = Okay   20 or below = You need a bit more practice.
Look at the Help suggestions in the Checkpoint.</td></tr>
</table>

CHECKPOINT

How confident do you feel about what you've learnt and practised? Tick the appropriate boxes.

				Help
Grammar focus: Second conditional *If I found a job in America, I'd move there.*	☐	☐	☐	► Pocket Grammar, pages (30) **31**
Vocabulary: Homes and what's in them, domestic chores	☐	☐	☐	► Vocabulary, page 105
How to say it: Likes and dislikes	☐	☐	☐	► Functions bank, page 113

Personal diary Write about your last lesson.

In Unit 3, we talked about . . .

Tips for learners Understanding new words in texts

If you are reading something and you see a word that you have never seen before and think you don't understand – don't panic! Asking yourself these two questions could help:

1 Is this word really very important? For example: *She just loves fattening desserts – and she immediately ordered a* **spotted dick** *from the menu.* You probably don't know exactly what a 'spotted dick' is. Never mind – you can assume that it is a dessert with a lot of calories in it. If you're *really* interested, you can look it up in a dictionary later.

2 Can I work out what it means? For example, in the text about Wakamaru you saw this: *... and runs on batteries that it* **recharges** *by itself.* Perhaps you can work out the meaning of *recharge* like this: I know what batteries are, I know that you can buy batteries, use batteries and recycle batteries. What else can I do with them? Ah yes – I can recharge some batteries and use them again.

Try these two strategies *before* you open your dictionary or ask another person!

Before you go on to Unit 4, try to find time to do the ***Getting ready*** page.

The world of work

1 What's it all about?

You saw this advertisement in the Evening Standard (a London daily newspaper) last week:

Top London hotel near Hyde Park is looking for a full-time **receptionist**, male or female, 25–40 years old, good spoken English (mother tongue unimportant), willing to work evenings and weekends. One month trial period, then permanent contract. Must have basic computer skills and some hotel experience. Accommodation available to single person, sorry not to a couple. Salary negotiable.
Contact: Box 0379, Evening Standard

Work with a partner. Decide which of these statements are true, false or not known from the information in the ad.

	true	not true	don't know
1 It is a 5-star hotel.	☐	☐	☐
2 The job is for 22 hours a week.	☐	☐	☐
3 A man or woman could get the job.	☐	☐	☐
4 The new receptionist must be British.	☐	☐	☐
5 The new receptionist must work every weekend.	☐	☐	☐
6 The job is only for a month.	☐	☐	☐
7 The new receptionist must have a computer at home.	☐	☐	☐
8 It is important that this is not the applicant's first hotel job.	☐	☐	☐
9 Only a single person can apply for the job.	☐	☐	☐
10 A single receptionist can live in the hotel.	☐	☐	☐
11 The salary is above average.	☐	☐	☐
12 People who are interested should write a letter to the hotel.	☐	☐	☐

2   Ask about the job

Work with a partner. Ask and answer questions beginning with
   Where?   *What?*   *When?*   *Who?*   *How long?*   *How much?*
about the job described in the job advert.

3   Contacting the Corus Hotel

Which word in the ad tells you that you should contact the hotel by letter if you're interested in the job?

....

Work in small groups or with a partner. Choose one expression from each of these boxes to put in your short letter.

1 ☐ Dear Sir or Madam,
   ☐ Dear Park Hotel,
   ☐ Dear Sirs,

2 ☐ What a great ad!
   ☐ I thought I'd get in touch …
   ☐ I'm writing about your …

3 ☐ I'm very interested in … because …
   ☐ I want …
   ☐ I think you should know that I …

4 ☐ I'm definitely the best person …
   ☐ I have had some experience of …
   ☐ I'm not sure if I can do the job, but …

5 ☐ I'll phone you on Friday to …
   ☐ Please contact me …
   ☐ I hope to hear from you about …

6 ☐ Yours sincerely,
   ☐ Yours faithfully,
   ☐ All the best,

🔊 **T 10**   A careers adviser is speaking to some young people about how to write a formal letter in answer to an advertisement in the newspaper. Listen to what she says.

Did you make the right choices above? According to the adviser, where should you put some additional information in your letter?
What sort of additional information should you put there?

You are interested in the job in London.
Work with a partner.
Write a short letter to the *Corus Hotel* as a reaction to their advertisement.

Exchange letters with another pair. Read their letter and underline anything you think could be better.

Have a look at your letters together. Discuss any changes. Ask your teacher for help if you aren't sure. Then finalise your letter.

4 🔊 T 11 **Making an appointment**

Listen to the telephone conversation. Someone is making an appointment to go to the hotel for an interview with the manager. Number these expressions in the order that you hear them.

- ☐ Would (... time ...) suit you?
- ☐ Oh sorry, no – I'm afraid that isn't possible for me.
- ☐ How about on (... day ...)?
- ☐ Yes, that would be fine.
- ☐ Could you be here on (... day ...) at (... time ...)?
- ☐ What time exactly?
- ☐ I'm afraid I can't make it in the morning.
- ☐ Would the afternoon be convenient for you?

Underline the expressions that were used by the hotel manager.

🔊 T 12 Listen again and check your answers.

5 **Your telephone call**

Work with a partner. One of you is the manager of a hotel, and the other has seen your advert and wants to make an appointment for an interview.
Plan the telephone call. Use all of the expressions in task 4. You can listen to the recorded telephone conversation again if you want to.

Now join another pair. Sit back to back with your partner, and 'perform' your telephone call to the others.

6 **What are your questions?**

Imagine that you are going for an interview for the job of receptionist at the *Corus Hotel* in London. Brainstorm with your class, and prepare the questions that you think you should ask at the interview.

7 **A different job**

Work with a partner. Choose one of these jobs:
- *gardener*
- *au-pair*
- *substitute grandma / grandad*
- *waiter / waitress*
- *street interviewer*
- *tourist guide*

One of you is the employer and the other is the potential employee. Think about the interview and plan your questions (don't let your partner see the questions). When you are ready, act out your interview for the rest of the class. You don't have to tell the truth!

8 **Discuss**

What experience have you had of job interviews?

If you had to give a school-leaver some tips about going for an interview what advice would you give?

Vocabulary (page 27)

Read the advertisement and the questions on page 27 again. Now write in as many of these words as you can without looking back at page 27.

1 The *Corus Hotel* put an .... in the newspaper.

2 A job that is about 40 hours a week is a .... job.

3 The language you grew up speaking is your ....

4 .... = not important

5 A time when you can try the job to see if you and it are okay is a .... period.

6 A document that you and an employer sign if you take a job is called a ....

7 The time you spent doing a job and what you learnt is your ....

8 This hotel can offer ...., perhaps just a room, to a single person.

9 If something e.g. the salary, can be discussed then it is ....

10 A person who answers the ad and asks for the job is an ....

If you can't remember all the words, look back and find the missing ones.

Vocabulary (pages 28–29)

choice [tʃɔɪs] Wahl
convenient [kən'viːnɪənt] passend, günstig
definitely ['defənətlɪ] bestimmt, definitiv, ein-
  deutig
experience [ɪk'spɪərɪəns] Erfahrung
get in touch [get ɪn 'tʌtʃ] jemanden kontaktieren,
  sich bei jemandem melden

I'm afraid I can't … [aɪm ə'freɪd aɪ ˌkɑːnt]
  ich fürchte, ich kann nicht …, leider kann ich
  nicht …
imagine [ɪ'mædʒɪn] sich vorstellen
perform [pə'fɔːm] aufführen, durchführen
school-leaver [ˌskuːl 'liːvə] Schulabgänger
waiter / waitress ['weɪtə / 'weɪtrəs] Kellner/in

Now you can do the following things in the world of work. You can:
✔ read and understand a simple job advertisement
✔ write a short semi-formal letter
✔ make an appointment on the telephone
✔ plan and ask questions to a potential employer
✔ give a younger, less-experienced person some tips about going to interviews.

Personal diary **Write about your last lesson.**

p. 93

Secret Agent 007

James Bond was created by the author Ian Fleming in 1953. The first James Bond film, *Dr. No* starring Sean Connery as 007, was made in 1962. There are now twenty James Bond films, and many people still think that Sean Connery played the part more convincingly than all the other actors who followed him. But even Sean Connery wasn't exactly like Ian Fleming's famous spy:

Ian Fleming's James Bond, described in 1953:
Age: 30s
Eyes: blue   Hair: black
Weight: 76 kg   Height: 1.82 m

Sean Connery as James Bond in 1962:
Age: 32
Eyes: brown   Hair: dark brown
Weight: 85 kg   Height: 1.89 m

Daniel Craig was chosen to be the sixth James Bond in 2005. At 1 metre 82 – exactly the height that Ian Fleming gave in his description – he is shorter than all the Bonds who went before him ... and, unlike all the others, he's blonde! 🔊 **L 16**

There are now 20 James Bond films, and more than half the world's population has seen one. Why do you think they are so popular? How many have you seen?

☐ none   ☐ a few
☐ a lot   ☐ all of them

Sean Connery as 007, 1983

Adjectives ▶ PG, page 34;
Adverbs ▶ PG, page 35

Are these sentences true (T) or false (F)?
☐ Daniel Craig is the tallest James Bond.
☐ Daniel Craig isn't as tall as Sean Connery.
☐ Sean Connery is lighter than Ian Fleming's 007.
☐ Many people still think that nobody has played 007 as convincingly as Sean Connery.

🔑 **page 93**

Daniel Craig, the sixth James Bond

4 Entertainment

1 Chat

What's your favourite way of spending your free time? Talk about free evenings and weekends in summer and winter.

2 Vocabulary check: Your free time

Underline the places that you can find in the area where you live:

bar	disco	theatre	cinema	stadium	restaurant
nightclub	concert hall	opera house	sports centre	fitness centre	evening school

Now tick (✔) the places that you sometimes go to (maybe only once or twice a year), and double tick (✔✔) the places that you go to regularly (at least once a month). Put a cross next to the places that you never go to. Then compare lists with a partner.

3 T 13 How to say it: Invitations

Listen to four people inviting someone to go out with them. In which conversation was the invitation

a) accepted very enthusiastically? ☐

b) neither accepted nor refused? ☐

c) refused rather sadly? ☐

d) refused angrily? ☐

T 14 Listen again. In which conversation did you hear these ways of inviting people?

e) Would you like to … ? ☐

f) I was wondering if you'd like to … ☐

g) I'd like to invite you to … ☐

h) Why don't you … ? ☐

Look at the *Functions bank* on pages 113 and 114. Choose one expression that you can use to accept and one to refuse an invitation.

Work in groups of three. Take it in turns to invite the other two people in the group. One of the two should accept the invitation, the other should refuse it politely and give a reason.

4 Adjectives and adverbs

In exercise 3 you saw these adverbs.

a) He accepted **enthusiastically**.

b) She refused **angrily**.

c) She refused rather **sadly**.

Write in the adjectives that the above adverbs come from:

a) **He** was very .... when he heard about the invitation.

b) **She** was very .... towards him when she refused his invitation.

c) **She** was very .... because she had to refuse his invitation.

Complete the sentence: *She works very …* with the adverbs made from:
a) *enthusiastic*, b) *bad*, c) *careful*, d) *fast*, e) *good*, f) *happy*, g) *hard*, h) *slow*.
Say the sentences aloud, e.g. *She works very enthusiastically*.

Which three adverbs don't end with *-ly*? ....

5 Grammar focus: **Comparatives** and **superlatives** ▶ LS, page 34

Daniel Craig was **older than** Sean Connery was when he became 007.
Daniel Craig isn't **as tall as** Sean Connery.
Sean Connery acted **more convincingly than** the other 007 actors, and he was **more attractive** than them, too. (A matter of opinion!)
Daniel Craig is **the shortest** 007 ever, at 1 metre 82!

Which was **the most popular** James Bond film? Which was **the least popular**?

Which word is the only adverb in this box? ....

5a Comparing people in your class

Compare yourself with other people in your class. Write two sentences on a piece of paper:
My hair is (long / short / dark / light / curly / straight) than X's hair.
I am (young / old / light / heavy / tall / short) than X.

Give the papers to your teacher. He/She will read some of the sentences to you. Can you guess who wrote them?

5b Comparing past James Bonds

Work with a partner. Find out more about the five actors who played James Bond before 2005. **Partner A**, look at page 89. **Partner B**, look at page 91.

5c The James Bond chain

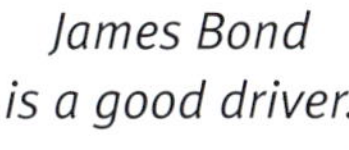

Make chains like this about James Bond.
Start with *a fast driver, usually a careful driver, sometimes a careless driver, sometimes a dangerous driver, never a slow driver, sometimes an aggressive driver.*

🔊 T 15 Listen and discuss

Listen to two friends talking about films. What sort of films does he like best? What sort does she like best?
(biographical, cartoon, comedy, detective, documentary, horror, romantic, science fiction, thriller, war)

What sort of TV or cinema films do you like best?

Cities usually offer a wide choice of entertainment to visitors. Talk about some cities (e.g. London, New York, Moscow, Dresden, Rome, …) and say what would you choose to do there on an evening out.

Language study

Adjectives and adverbs

Adjektive bestimmen Substantive näher, **Adverbien** Verben.

Identify those four types of words in these sentences.

He's a good actor.   noun: ....   adjective: ....

He can act well.   verb: ....   adverb: ....

Die meisten Adverbien werden gebildet, indem man *-ly* an das Adjektiv anhängt: *slow – slowly*.
Es gibt aber auch ein paar unregelmäßige Formen: *good – well, fast – fast, hard – hard*.

So können Sie mehr über Substantive sagen:

	adjective	comparative	superlative
short adjectives	It's old. It's big.	It's older than … It's bigger than …	It's the oldest. It's the biggest.
long adjectives	It's expensive. It's interesting.	It's more expensive than … It's less interesting than …	It's the most expensive. It's the least interesting.
irregular forms	It's good. It's bad.	It's better than … It's worse than …	It's the best. It's the worst.

Sie können Dinge auch vergleichen, indem Sie *as … as* verwenden: *His car wasn't as expensive as mine.*
Dieser Satz bedeutet: His car was ☐ more expensive than mine.
☐ the same price as mine.
☐ cheaper than mine.

So können Sie mehr über Verben sagen:

	adverb	comparative
regular	He writes carefully.	He writes more carefully than his boss.
irregular	He cooks well / badly. He works hard / fast.	He cooks better / worse than his wife. He works harder / faster than his boss.

Sie können Handlungen auch vergleichen, indem Sie *as … as* verwenden:
John doesn't work as hard as his boss.
Dieser Satz bedeutet: ☐ John works harder than his boss.
☐ John's boss works harder than John.

🗝 **page 93**

---

info

➤ **Everything on standby** In Britain, the government is concerned about people's televisions – not about how long they are on, but about the time when they are on standby. A TV on standby uses two-thirds of the electricity that it would use if it were on. And many people leave their televisions on standby all the time – even when they are away on holiday. Experts estimate that there will be about 74 million televisions in the UK by the year 2020 (that's more than the number of people). So the message to manufacturers is: produce televisions without a standby function. The message to the public is: until then … switch off!

🔊 **L 17**

1 Grammar: Adjectives and adverbs

Underline two <u>adjectives</u> and circle two (adverbs) in both of these short texts **(8 points)**.

1 He's a great actor. He speaks clearly and he always gets on well with all the actors. He's a good singer, too.

2 James Bond always drives fast and sometimes rather dangerously in his films. Of course, he always gets fast cars to drive, and – after all – who would want to see a 'careful' James Bond?

Write in the missing words here.

3 My neighbour's car is faster .... mine, and it's also much .... expensive to run.

4 His car isn't .... interesting as my car. Mine is .... beautiful car in town – it's pink.

Now complete these sentences with the correct form of the word *bad*.

5 My neighbour is a really .... cook.

He cooks so .... that nobody can eat

his food. His soups are .... than

mine, and his spaghetti bolognese is the

.... I've ever eaten!

> **1** point for each correct answer — My score: **17**

2 Vocabulary

What do you want to know?

1 How old is he?   I want to know his ....

2 How heavy is he? I want to know his ....

3 How tall is he?   I want to know his ....

Complete the expressions for these places where you can go in your free time:

4 fitness ....   6 evening ....

5 concert ....   7 opera ....

> **1** point for each correct answer — My score: **7**

3 Pronunciation

Underline the stressed <u>syllable</u> in each of these adjectives:

1 attractive   4 dangerous
2 popular   5 unhappy
3 aggressive   6 convincing

L 18 Listen and check your answers.

> **1** point for each correct answer — My score: **6**

4 L 19 Listening

Listen to these short parts of telephone conversations. The people are all talking about where they went last night. They didn't all go to the cinema – where did they go?

1 ....   4 ....

2 ....   5 ....

3 ....   6 ....

> **1** point for each correct answer — My score: **6**

5 How to say it: Invitations

Use the words given to complete the two reactions to this invitation:

Would you like to have dinner with me on Friday?

1 *afraid – but – can't – love – much – yes – you – would*

a) ...., I .... Thank .... very ....

b) I'd .... to, ... I'm .... I ....

2 *at – be – I'd – nice – pity – sorry – to – weekend*

a) Oh, that's .... Thanks, ... love .... come.

b) I'm ...., that's a .... I'll .... away .... the ....

> **1** point for each correct answer — My score: **4**

p. 94

p. 106

www

Over to you
My total score: **40**

40–36 = Excellent   **35–31** = Very good   **30–26** = Good
25–21 = Okay   **20** or below = You need a bit more practice.
Look at the **Help** suggestions in the **Checkpoint**.

CHECKPOINT

How confident do you feel about what you've learnt and practised? Tick the appropriate boxes.

Help

Grammar focus: Adjectives and adverbs, comparatives and superlatives
► Pocket Grammar, pages (34, 35) **36**

Vocabulary: Places of entertainment, describing people
► Vocabulary, page 106

How to say it: Invitations
► Functions bank, page 113

Personal diary Write about your last lesson.

Tips for learners Being polite

The British are often (not always!) very polite when they speak to people. Foreigners may sometimes sound a bit impolite in English, even if they don't want to be impolite at all. Here are a few tips:

- The word *please* is a key word in English. If you say *two beers, please* in a pub, *sausage and chips, please* in a restaurant and a *return ticket, please* at the station … you will get friendlier reactions from people.
- Short answers are fine, but *yes* and *no* are too short – they sound abrupt and unfriendly. Try to use answers like *Yes, I do* or *No, I haven't* instead.
- If you want to ask a stranger something, or if you want to interrupt a person to speak to them, don't just start talking – begin with *Excuse me, …*.
- And last but not least, remember to say *Thank you* – and when somebody says 'thank you' to you, smile and say *You're welcome*.

Before you go on to Unit 5, try to find time to do the **Getting ready** page.   

▶ **In this unit, you're going to ...**

- talk about the building where you live and its surroundings
- focus on how *some, any, much, many, a lot, a little* and *a few* are used
- practise talking about needs and wishes
- review vocabulary of colours and furnishings

My home is my castle

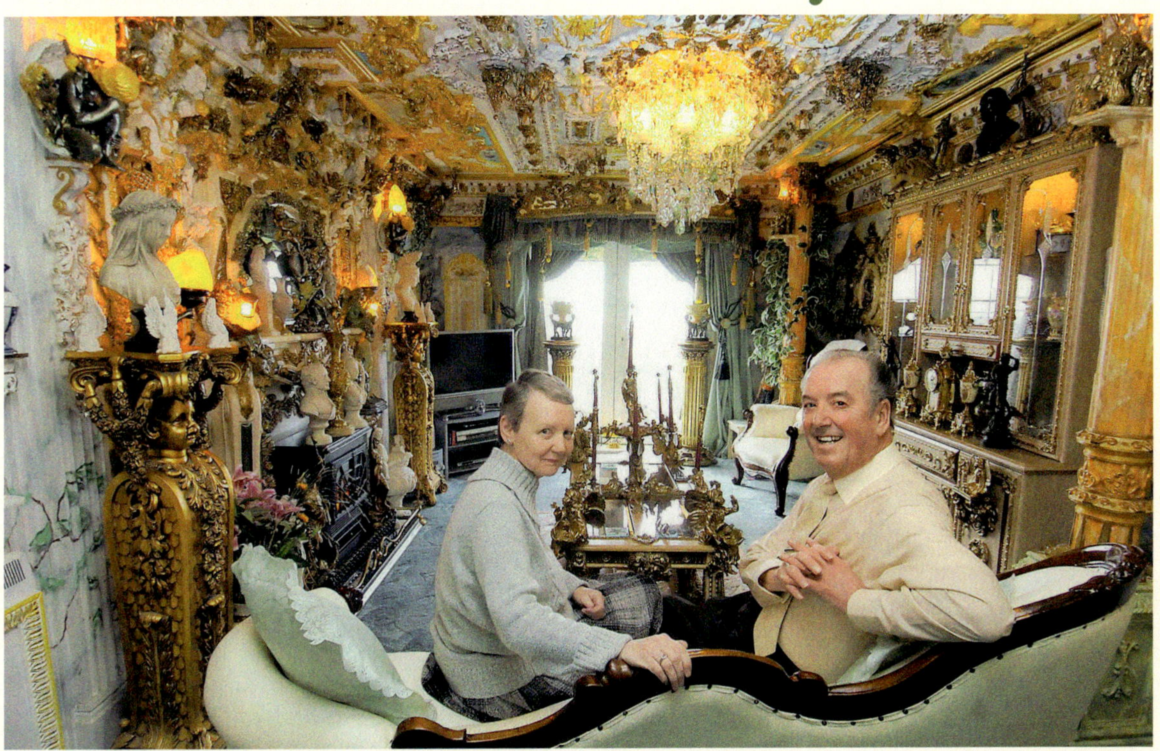

In the case of Dennis and Norma Nelems, the saying should really be 'My home is my palace'. When they moved into their new retirement flat, Dennis hated the beige carpets and white walls so much that he decided to change things ... completely. They haven't got any posters or bookshelves on their walls like many people have, but they haven't got any free wall space either. What they have got is a living room that can only be described as a baroque masterpiece. It's filled with angels, cherubs, baroque pillars and Michelangelo-style paintings. The only sign of the 21st century is the TV in the corner.

People often ask Dennis how much it cost them to decorate the room and how many hours of hard work he invested in it. He proudly reports, "I worked on this room for six years, and the total cost was about £30,000. Now that I'm retired, I need to have something to do ... so I might transform the bedrooms next!" Luckily, Norma is perfectly happy with that. She says that she definitely wouldn't want anything to be different.

🔊 L 20

Would you be happy to let Dennis redesign your living room? Why (not)?

How much / How many ▶ PG, page 32

Preview

Write *much* or *many* in the gaps.

How .... money did Dennis spend on his living room?

How .... hours did he invest in the work?

How .... angels are there in his living room?

How .... free wall space is there in the room?   🔑 page 94

5 A place to live

1 Chat

Would you like to have your English lessons in Dennis and Norma Nelems' living room? Why (not)?
If you could change the appearance and style of the room you are in now, what would you and/or your teacher like to be different?

2 Vocabulary check: Colours

Work with a partner. What are the most dominant colours in the Nelems' living room on page 37?

Which words do you need to express the difference between these two blues?

.... blue ▮   .... blue ▮

How many different colours can you find in your class? Describe where in the room those colours are, e.g. *The curtains / walls are beige. My pullover is dark green.*

3 🔊 T 16 The ideal building

Richard and Helen, some young friends of the Nelems, don't really like the baroque living room very much. They'd prefer to live in a modern flat. They're talking about a new building project in their town, Bristol. Listen. Which of these things are planned in the project (✔) and which aren't (✘)?

☐ lift
☐ restaurants
☐ offices
☐ supermarket
☐ sports facilities
☐ guest rooms
☐ leisure facilities
☐ rooftop swimming pool

Check your answers with a partner:
There is a / isn't a / are some / aren't any ...
Is there a ... / Are there any ...?

Can you remember what they said?
Is there any real grass on the roof?
☐ Yes, there is some real grass on the roof.
☐ No, there isn't any real grass on the roof.

www.uniform.net

4 Grammar focus: Countables and uncountables ▶ LS, page 40

Talking about countables

Is there a lift?	There is a lift.	There isn't a lift.
Are there any offices?	There are some offices.	There aren't any offices.
How many offices are there?	One. / Only a few. / A lot.	None.

Talking about uncountables

Is there any grass on the roof?	There is some grass.	There isn't any real grass.
How much grass is there?	Only a little. / A lot.	None.

Countable or uncountable?
Look at the *Preview* on page 37.   Which nouns are countable? ....

Which are uncountable? ....

4a Countable or uncountable?

Make two columns on a piece of paper:
countable and *uncountable*. Your teacher is going
to read a list of 16 nouns to you. Write them in
the correct column (8 in each). Teacher: please
look at page 96.

4b What is there?

Circle the (uncountable) nouns and underline the
countable nouns.

candles	*Ikea* furniture	piano
free wall space	mirrors	posters
gold paint	natural light	TV

Make a question chain around the class. Ask:
Is there a …
Is there any …   *in the Nelems' living room?*
Are there any …

If the answer is *Yes*, ask another question with
How much … or *How many … .*

Now work with a partner. Ask about the above
things in his/her workplace, living room,
bathroom, bedroom, etc.

Choose one of your partner's answers that would
not be correct for you, e.g. *My partner has got
a … on her balcony, but I haven't got one on
mine.* Report this to the class.

4c Something, somewhere, someone

Work in groups of three.
One person (A) should choose a category: *a thing,
a place* or *a person*. The second person (B) should
choose: *positive, negative* or *question*.

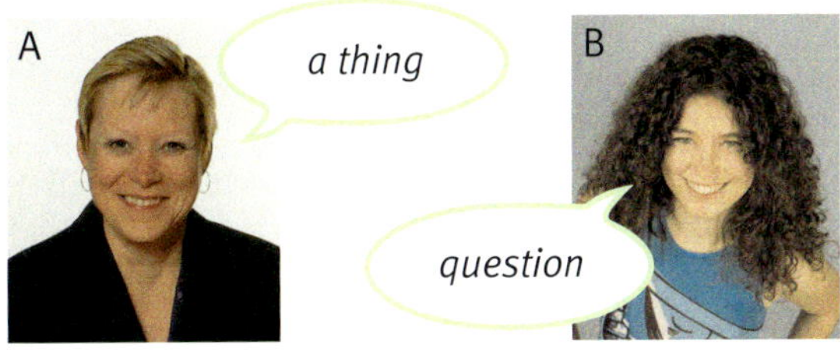

The third person (C) should make a sentence or
question:

Answer all the questions, too.

Words beginning with *some-* are used in
positive sentences.
Words beginning with *any-* are used in
negative sentences and questions.

5 How to say it: Needs and wishes

Richard and Helen used these expressions when they spoke about the building project. Which three
express a need (N) and which three express a wish (W)?

☐ The building must be …   ☐ If possible, there should be …   ☐ I'd prefer to …

☐ I'd rather have a … than a …   ☐ I definitely need to have …   ☐ My biggest 'must' is a …

Choose one 'need' and one 'wish' expression. You'll need to use these expressions in the next exercise.

 T 17 Listen and discuss

Richard and Helen, who you listened to before, have decided that they don't want to reserve a flat in the
new project. Listen to what they say about the position of their ideal flat. What do they mention?

Talk in groups about the things that are near your home and the views from your windows.

Now imagine that your group is going to build a place to live together. Everybody will have their own flat.
Can you agree on the top ten requirements – you've got plenty of money to spend! Remember – try to
use the expressions you chose in exercise 5.

Language study

Much, many, some, any, etc.

Die Menge oder Anzahl von etwas feststellen, das existiert oder verfügbar ist:

	question	answers				
Countable nouns	How **many** new houses are there?	A lot.	Not many.	A few.	One, two …	None.
Uncountable nouns	How **much** water is there?	A lot.	Not much.	A little.	A litre …	None.

Feststellen, ob etwas existiert oder verfügbar ist:

	question	positive	negative
Countable nouns	Is there **a** supermarket near your home? Are there **any** new flats in your town?	There's **a** small supermarket. There are **some** new houses.	There isn't **a** big supermarket. There aren't **any** new flats.
Uncountable nouns	Have you got **any** water in the fridge?	I've got **some** tap water.	I haven't got **any** mineral water.

Details über Orte, Menschen und Dinge feststellen:

Write the words *places*, *people* and *things* in the correct places in the first column.

………………	Did you buy **anything** yesterday?	I bought **something** for my son.	No, I didn't buy **anything**. Absolutely **nothing**.
………………	Did you go **anywhere** yesterday?	I went **somewhere** in the morning.	No, I didn't go **anywhere**. Absolutely **nowhere**.
………………	Did you meet **anyone** yesterday?	I met **someone** in the pub.	No, I didn't meet **anyone**. Absolutely **no one**.

page 94

info

Buying a house or flat in the UK In English streets you can often see 'for sale' signs outside houses. These signs tell you how you can contact the estate agent's (known as real estate offices in America). If you are interested in a house or flat, you can ask the estate agent to show you the property and if you decide that you want to buy it – you can make an offer to the person who is selling. It is usual to offer less than the price that was asked for and then some negotiations follow. Your next step (unless you can pay all the money immediately) is to arrange a mortgage with a bank or building society and deal with all the paperwork. In Scotland, the system is different. The person who is selling gives a 'not below' price – then everybody who is interested can make an offer above that price. The seller will, of course, accept the highest offer. The problem is that you don't know what other people have offered!

L 21

1 Grammar: *Some / any* etc.

Underline the eight **uncountable** nouns in this list:

advice	information	newspaper
bread	man	project
dollar	minute	question
furniture	money	time
help	news	word

Cross out the words that are **not** correct.

1 How *many / much* flats are there in the building? – Only a *little / a few / none*.
2 She'd like to see *a / any / some* trees from the window, but she can't see *anything / something* green at all.
3 She has got *a / any / some* balcony with *a little / any / a few* pots on it.
4 Her father gave her *an / many / some* advice about the plants – she doesn't understand very *many / much* about gardening.
5 Did she have to buy *a / some / any* furniture for her new flat? – Only *a few / a little*.
6 Did she look *somewhere / anywhere* else for a flat? No, *anywhere / nowhere* at all.

1 point for each correct answer (8 + 12)	My score:	20

2 Pronunciation

Read this text aloud. Find four pairs of words that sound the same but are written differently.

Richard and Helen bought a house last week. Helen says, "I really like our new house, I think we'll be very happy there." Richard is feeling a bit nervous because they haven't sold their old house yet. He says, "We don't want to stay here much longer. We can't have two houses! The new house is great. It isn't too far from the station and I'll be less than an hour from work." One man looked at the old house yesterday and they hope to hear from him very soon.

1 .... + ...   3 .... + ...
2 .... + ...   4 .... + ...

1 point for each correct pair	My score:	4

3 Vocabulary: Colours

Write the name of a colour in each gap.

1 as .... as the sky in summer
2 as .... as blood
3 as .... as a sunflower
4 as .... as grass
5 as .... as snow
6 as .... as a hazelnut

1 point for each correct answer	My score:	6

4 L 22 Listening

If you haven't read the *Info* section yet – go back and read it now. Then listen to the estate agent telling four potential clients about four properties that he has got for sale. Match each of the four clients to the type of property they are looking for.

☐ a flat   ☐ a house
☐ a bungalow   ☐ a shop with a flat
☐ a garage   above it

1 point for each correct answer	My score:	4

5 How to say it: Needs and wishes

Match the two parts of the sentences.

1 I'd rather
2 I'd prefer
3 If possible, it
4 The building must be
5 I really
6 My biggest 'must'

☐ a) should have a parking space.
☐ b) modern.
☐ c) need to have a lift.
☐ d) have a balcony than a garden.
☐ e) is a small balcony.
☐ f) to have a lovely view and no garden.

1 point for each correct answer	My score:	6

p. 94

p. 107

WWW

TYS, p. 81

Over to you
My total score: [ ] **40**

40–36 = Excellent   **35–31** = Very good   **30–26** = Good
25–21 = Okay   **20** or below = You need a bit more practice.
Look at the **Help** suggestions in the **Checkpoint**.

CHECKPOINT

How confident do you feel about what you've learnt and practised? Tick the appropriate boxes.

Help

Grammar focus: *Some, any, much, many,*
a lot, a little and *a few*
▸ Pocket Grammar,
   pages (32) **33**
Vocabulary: Colours and furnishings
▸ Vocabulary, page 107
How to say it: Needs and wishes
▸ Functions bank, page 114

Personal diary **Write about your last lesson.**

Tips for learners **How to help yourself if you don't understand**

Don't be too worried if you find that you don't always understand what other people say in English.
There are many different reasons why it is sometimes difficult to understand spoken language. These
reasons range from too much background noise to lack of concentration and from mumbling speakers
to over-specialised vocabulary. So what can you do?

- If you *know* that you haven't understood something, use one of the expressions listed for Unit 1 in the
  Functions bank (page 113). The person you are having a conversation with should be able to help you.
- It's a different problem if you *aren't sure* if you have understood or not. There are three golden rules
  here:
  a) Don't panic!
  b) Don't pretend that you have understood when you haven't.
  c) Ask checking questions to confirm the message, e.g. *Oh, you mean the restaurant behind the
     station, do you? / Oh, that's the bus stop outside the bookshop, isn't it?*
     Remember! It's better to be safe than sorry.

Before you go on to Unit 6, try to find time to do the **Getting ready** page.

In this unit, you're going to ...

- talk about sports and other leisure time activities
- focus on speaking about the past
  (*I played ..., I used to play ..., I have played ...*)
- practise making and reacting to suggestions
- review vocabulary about sport, and the names of countries and nationalities

Better times for bulls?

Bullfighting isn't as popular in Spain as it used to be. In fact, only a minority of the Spanish say that they are interested in it. The majority say that they aren't interested at all. Bullfighting has become politically incorrect. In 2003, Catalonia banned children under fourteen from bullrings, and is now thinking about banning *all* bullfights. Other parts of Spain may do the same in the future.

A lot of people find bullfighting too violent and that's the reason why so many multinational companies don't want to sponsor the sport – they don't want to harm their image. Very few people want to take their children or grandchildren to the bullring with them – as they used to do. Young people are more interested in other sports and leisure time activities.

This, of course, is bad news for the bullring owners. But they have already found some other ways of earning money by using the bullrings for different events. Many true fans of the drama, skill, romance and passion of the bullfight find it difficult, however, to accept the concerts, acrobatic acts and gift shops that have become part of many bullrings in the country. 🔊 L 23

Have you ever seen a bullfight? What other sports do you think are 'violent'?

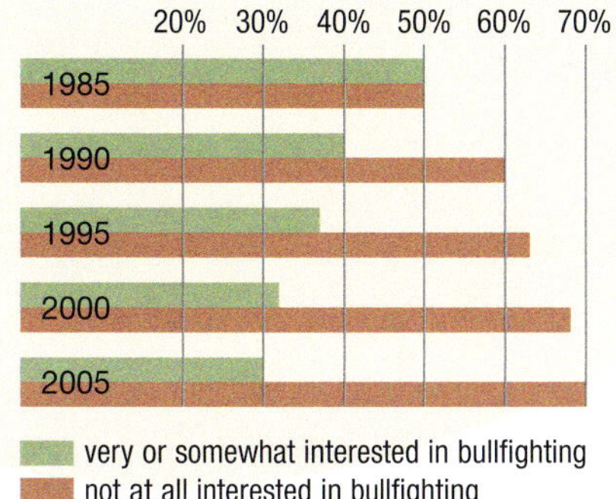

	20%	30%	40%	50%	60%	70%
1985						
1990						
1995						
2000						
2005						

🟩 very or somewhat interested in bullfighting
🟫 not at all interested in bullfighting

(surveys of 1,000 – 2,000 Spaniards)

Past simple ▶ PG, page 13; *Used to* ▶ PG, page 15; Present perfect simple ▶ PG, page 9

Preview

Bullfighting used to be very popular in Spain.
Was it very popular in the past? ☐ yes ☐ no
Is it very popular now? ☐ yes ☐ no

Gift shops have opened in many bullrings in Spain.
Do any gift shops exist in bullrings in Spain? ☐ yes ☐ no
Do we know exactly when they opened? ☐ yes ☐ no

🔑 **page 94**

6 Sport and leisure

1 Chat

Sport is a very popular leisure time activity – but not for everybody. Talk about other activities that people who you know do in their leisure time.

2 Ball sports

You need a ball to do all of these sports. Work with a partner. Complete the names of the sports by writing the correct vowels (a, e, i, o, u) in the gaps.

b __ s __ b __ l l   f ___ t b __ l l   t __ b l __ - t __ n n __ s

b __ s k __ t b __ l l   h __ c k __ y   t __ n n __ s

c r __ c k __ t   r __ g b y   v __ l l __ y b __ l l

Which of these sports can you see in the photos?

Divide your class into four groups. Each group should plan a short description of the job that **one** of these people does in the world of sport.

manager   referee   sponsor   trainer   sports reporter

Describe the job you chose to the others (don't mention the job). Match the descriptions to the jobs.

3 Vocabulary check: Countries and nationalities

One person should say the name of a country, e.g. *Italy*. Another person should say which sport they think the people there are keen on, e.g. *I think the Italians are keen on cycling.* You could talk about: *Canada, Australia, England, the USA, France, Germany, Austria, Brazil, China, Switzerland, …*

4 How to say it: Making and reacting to suggestions

Work in groups. Suggest different ways of completing the three reactions below.

1 **Shall we** go and see the tennis final tomorrow? – Oh, I'd rather not. I *(give an explanation)* …
2 **Let's** go to the cinema next week. – Yes, let's. Shall we *(make an additional suggestion)* …
3 **Why don't we** watch the quiz show on TV this evening? – Well actually, I'd prefer to watch *(suggest another programme)* …

Now work with a partner. Use the three expressions in bold to suggest some other leisure activities. Did your partner react positively to any of your suggestions?

5 🔊 T 18 A street interview

A local radio reporter interviewed a lot of people in the street about sport and their leisure time. Listen to what five of them said. Make notes about the sport that each person likes best. If they don't like sport very much, what do they prefer to do in their leisure time?

6 Grammar focus: Past simple, *used to* and present perfect simple ▸ LS, page 46

I **played** tennis **when** I was at school – now I enjoy watching it on TV. I last **saw** a match about a week **ago**.
My brother **used to hate** all sports **when** he was at school. He **didn't want** to compete all the time. He **spent** all his leisure time reading.
I'**ve never seen** a baseball match. **Have** you **ever seen** one? No, I **haven't**.

Which verbs are about all your life up to now?	☐ blue	☐ green
Which verbs are about a specific time in the past?	☐ blue	☐ green

6a Verb forms

Your teacher is going to read out a list of ten verbs that have irregular past simple forms.
Write them down, e.g. *come – came, do – did*. Teacher: please look at page 96.

Then work with a partner and add the verb form that you have to use in the present perfect simple, e.g. *come – came – come, do – did – done*.

Ask your partner three or four questions beginning with *Have you ever …?*, using verbs from your list.

6b Your leisure time

Work in small groups. Tell the people in your group as much as you can about sports, leisure interests and hobbies in your life. Try to make sentences with these words: *ago, never, used to, just, when, already, not yet*. Ask each other questions with *Have you ever …?* Look at the *Grammar focus* and the *Remember* box for help.

Remember

I've **just** started playing squash.
(not *I just started*)
She's **already** done her homework.
(not *She already did*)
They haven't finished their project **yet**.
(not *They didn't finish*)

6c Find someone who

Work with a partner. **Partner A**, look at page 90. **Partner B**, look at page 92.

🔊 T 19 Listen and discuss

Another woman who was interviewed by the radio reporter had some very strong opinions about sport. Listen to what she says. What aspects does she mention?

Which of her opinions do you agree / disagree with?

Now go on to talk about how you *really* like to spend your leisure time and how that has changed over the years.

Language study

Past simple

1 Die **einfache Vergangenheit** wird verwendet, um von etwas zu sprechen, das zu einem bestimmten Zeitpunkt in der Vergangenheit stattgefunden hat.

2 Die einfache Vergangenheit von *to be* hat zwei Formen: *was(n't)* und *were(n't)*.

3 Andere Verben haben nur eine Form, die in allen Personen identisch ist.

   Complete these questions and answer them, using the correct forms of *be* and *go:*

   a) Where .... you yesterday evening? I .... at home.

   b) Where .... you .... last weekend? I .... to London.

      I .... to Bristol.

4 *Used to* stellt eine Besonderheit dar – es steht immer vor einem anderen Verb,
   z.B. *Maria used to play hockey.*
   Auch die Bedeutung ist eine besondere – wir erfahren, dass Maria heute nicht mehr Hockey spielt.

Present perfect simple

1 Die **einfache Form der vollendeten Gegenwart** wird verwendet, um über Dinge zu sprechen, die sich in einem Zeitraum ereignet haben, der bis an die Gegenwart heranreicht,
   z.B. *today*, *this week*, *this year* usw.

2 Sie wird auch verwendet, um auszudrücken, dass etwas zu einem unbestimmten Zeitpunkt im Leben stattgefunden hat, z.B. *I've been to New York twice. I've already seen that film.*

3 Man kann sie auch für Aussagen über das gesamte Leben verwenden,
   z.B. *I've never understood cricket. I've always wanted to see a cricket match.*

! Den Unterschied im Gebrauch der **einfachen Vergangenheit** und der **einfachen Form der vollendeten Gegenwart** können Sie an diesen Sätzen gut erkennen.

Write these verbs in the gaps: *been*, *bought*, *has*, *have*, *haven't*, *saw*, *seen*, *sold*, *went*.

c) I .... my brother last week, but I .... him this week.

d) He .... to America in 1995, but he .... never .... to Canada.

e) They .... their old car three months ago and they .... just

   .... a new one.

page 94

info

The team spirit A generation or two ago, sport was the main area in which the word 'team' was used. But 'team spirit' can now mean the way people communicate with and understand each other, especially at work. Big companies often send their employees on special *bonding* or *team building* courses or seminars. This can be very positive, but can also be traumatic when people have to face situations that they don't know how to deal with. They also have to learn to trust, respect and help each other. One thing is certain, on a team building course people often learn unexpected things about themselves and their colleagues.

 L 24

1 Grammar: Past simple, *used to* and present perfect simple

Match the parts of the sentences and questions.

1 She has just ☐   a) a year ago.
2 She hasn't ☐   b) done it.
3 Why did ☐   c) to do it.
4 Has she ☐   d) done it yet.
5 She didn't ☐   e) never done it.
6 She used ☐   f) ever done it?
7 She last did it ☐   g) she do it?
8 She has ☐   h) do it.

Write the correct form of the verb in brackets.

9 She first *(go)* .... to Paris when she was 18.

10 She *(never see)* .... any other French cities.

11 She *(leave)* .... her old job a month ago.

12 She *(not like)* .... her old boss.

13 She *(just start)* .... a new job.

14 She *(already meet)* .... her new colleagues.

15 She *(not be)* .... late for work yet.

> **1** point for each correct answer   My score: **15**

2 Vocabulary: Nationalities

Five nationalities from this list of countries end in *-ian*. Write them down.

Germany, Austria, France, Australia, Brazil, England, Italy, Canada, Spain, USA

....

....

....

> **1** point for each correct answer   My score: **5**

3 Pronunciation

Underline the word in the first part of the sentence that is stressed.

1 They used to play tennis – but they've never played squash.
2 They used to play tennis – but now they watch it on TV.
3 They used to play tennis – but their son didn't.
4 They didn't use to play tennis – but they do now.
5 They used to play tennis – but they don't anymore.

🔊 **L 25** Listen and check your answers.

> **1** point for each correct answer   My score: **5**

4 How to say it: Making and reacting to suggestions

Complete these suggestions.

1 S.......... w.......... stay at home?

2 L.......... stay at home.

3 W.......... d.......... w.......... stay at home?

🔊 **L 26** Now listen to some people reacting to suggestions. Which word did you hear in each reaction? Number the words below 1–7.

☐ a) love ✔ ✘
☐ b) rather ✔ ✘
☐ c) let's ✔ ✘
☐ d) prefer ✔ ✘
☐ e) actually ✔ ✘
☐ f) sorry ✔ ✘
☐ g) idea ✔ ✘

🔊 **L 27** Listen again. Did the people agree to go to the cinema or not? Circle ✔ or ✘.

> **1** point for each correct answer   My score: **10**

5 🔊 L 28 Listening

Listen to five people speaking about their jobs in the world of sports. Number these jobs 1–5.

☐ manager   ☐ referee   ☐ sponsor
☐ sports reporter   ☐ trainer

> **1** point for each correct answer   My score: **5**

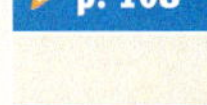
p. 94

p. 108

WWW

Over to you
My total score: [ ] / **40**

40–36 = Excellent   **35–31** = Very good   **30–26** = Good
25–21 = Okay   **20** or below = You need a bit more practice.
Look at the **Help** suggestions in the **Checkpoint**.

CHECKPOINT

How confident do you feel about what you've learnt and practised? Tick the appropriate boxes.

Help

Grammar focus: The past (*I played ...,*
I used to play ... , I have played ...)
▶ Pocket Grammar,
  pages (13, 15, 9) **16**
Vocabulary: Sport, countries, nationalities
▶ Vocabulary, page 108
How to say it: Making and reacting to
suggestions
▶ Functions bank, page 114

Personal diary Write about your last lesson.

Tips for learners Learning words

There are several things that you could do to help you to remember words:
- You could write new words on post-its and stick them somewhere where you will see them every day. When you see them, say them aloud and think about the meaning.
- Or you could write the new words on cards and take them with you when you go on a bus or a train. Then you can learn the words while you're travelling. Write the English on one side and the German on the other, then you can test yourself.
- You could keep a vocabulary book. In this you could write down the new and important words in whichever way you like best – a page per letter of the alphabet, a page per topic (e.g. food words, sport words) or a page per lesson.
- But don't forget the vocabulary pages in this course book (pages 103–112) where you can highlight the words that you want to learn.

Before you go on to Unit 7, try to find time to do the *Getting ready* page.

The world of travel

1 A competition

A large travel office is holding a competition. All you have to do is answer some questions about Texas.
The prize is, of course, a holiday in Texas.
Your teacher has got the quiz questions. Teacher: please look at page 96.
Work in groups of four. Listen to the questions and decide on the answers together.

People

1 ☐ Abraham Lincoln	☐ John F. Kennedy
2 ☐ Bill Clinton	☐ George W. Bush
3 ☐ Clyde (partner of Bonnie)	☐ Al Capone
4 ☐ chicken farmers	☐ cowboys

Places

5 ☐ Alaska	☐ Texas
6 ☐ Dallas	☐ Austin
7 ☐ Mexico	☐ New Mexico
8 ☐ Alcatraz	☐ The Alamo

Things

9 ☐ the Pacific Ocean	☐ the Gulf of Mexico
10 ☐ lobster	☐ chili
11 ☐ American football	☐ soccer
12 ☐ gold	☐ oil

2 🔊 T 20 **And now – the answers**

Two friends have decided that the best way to win the 'Texas' competition is to check their answers with an American friend. Listen and check your answers to the competition questions.

🔊 T 21 Listen again. Make notes on the information you heard about Abraham Lincoln, Bill Clinton, Al Capone and Alcatraz. Then compare your notes with a partner.

3 **A place to stay in Texas**

Texas is a very varied state – with huge cities, very small towns, sea, a national park and desert. San Antonio is a popular destination for visitors – especially those that are interested in the history of Texas. One of the nicest places to stay is an old hotel called the *Menger*. Work with a partner. Read this information about the *Menger* and answer the questions below.

WELCOME TO THE HISTORIC MENGER HOTEL!

Built in 1859, this beautiful structure has become an important part of San Antonio's history. The hotel is located downtown, immediately adjacent to both the *Alamo* and the *Rivercenter Mall*.

In addition to its significance as a historical landmark, the **MENGER** offers unparalleled amenities including: The famous Colonial Room Restaurant, the Menger Bar, downtown San Antonio's largest heated swimming pool, a full service spa, fitness room, and jacuzzi, just to name a few. We look forward to serving you at the **MENGER**!!

Free High Speed Internet access in all our guestrooms. Wireless access in the lobby area.

Airport Shuttle Service is provided by SATrans and picks up every 30 minutes. Tickets may be purchased at the airport terminal.

1 Underline the words in the text that mean the same as the following:
   a) *building*, b) *town centre*, c) *next to*, d) *importance*, e) *facilities*, f) *hotel entrance hall*, g) *bought*.
2 How long has the Menger been serving visitors in San Antonio?
3 Which two things do you think tourists would go and see in San Antonio?
4 Which two of the hotel's amenities would be most important for you?
5 What's the difference between the Internet access in the guestrooms and in the lobby?
6 Do visitors have to take a taxi to the airport when they leave? How can they get there?

4 Across the Atlantic

There were a few differences between American English and British English in the *Menger Hotel's* description:
downtown (AmE) = *town centre* (BE)
center (AmE) = *centre* (BE)
mall (AmE) = *shopping centre* (BE).
A lot of American English words have crossed the Atlantic and are used in British English today – but there are still some differences.

Work with a partner. Match the American and British words. The American words that are often also used in British English (with the same meaning) are marked with *.

1 hi*	☐ lift
2 cab*	☐ film
3 bill	☐ shop
4 pants	☐ flat
5 color	☐ taxi
6 store*	☐ chips
7 check	☐ hello
8 movie*	☐ toilet
9 closet	☐ centre
10 center	☐ theatre
11 theater	☐ colour
12 elevator	☐ cinema
13 first floor	☐ car park
14 bathroom	☐ trousers
15 apartment*	☐ fortnight
16 kilometer	☐ bank note
17 parking lot	☐ cupboard
18 French fries*	☐ kilometre
19 fourteen days	☐ ground floor
20 movie theater	☐ bill (restaurant)

What rule can you make about the spelling of words that mean the same and look *almost* the same in American and British English?

5 🔊 T 22 A weekend at the Menger

Listen to the telephone conversation between a travel agent and a man who wants to reserve a hotel at the *Menger*. Write the missing words in these sentences that are typically used on the phone.

1 Good morning. Can ....?

2 Hold .... , please.

3 I'm sorry, the ....'s ....

4 Oh, just .... , it's .... now.

5 I'll .... you ....

6 Hello, ... Sally.

7 I'll .... you ....

🔊 T 23 Listen again. Write down all the information you know about the room that Mr Jackson would like to book.

Now work in groups of three. Two of you work at the travel agency and one of you is Mr Jackson. Reconstruct the telephone conversation using the expressions above and the hotel vocabulary that you wrote down.

6 A postcard home

Work with a partner. Imagine that you are both in San Antonio for a weekend. Write a short text for a postcard that you want to send to a friend back home. Tell your friend a bit about San Antonio and the *Menger* Hotel. Don't forget – a postcard isn't very big!

Exchange 'postcards' with another pair and read what they have written. Do this until you have read all the postcards in the class.

Vocabulary (pages 49–51)

amenities [ə'mi:nətɪz] Annehmlichkeiten, Zusatzleistungen
competition [ˌkɒmpə'tɪʃən] Wettbewerb
cross [krɒs] überqueren
desert ['dezət] Wüste
destination [ˌdestɪ'neɪʃən] Ziel
difference ['dɪfrəns] Unterschied
fortnight ['fɔːtnaɪt] vierzehn Tage
history ['hɪstərɪ] Geschichte
huge [hjuːdʒ] riesig

imagine [ɪ'mædʒɪn] sich vorstellen
lobster ['lɒbstə] Hummer
popular ['pɒpjələ] beliebt
reconstruct [ˌriːkən'strʌkt] rekonstruieren
serve [sɜːv] bedienen, dienen
still [stɪl] noch
travel agent ['trævl ˌeɪdʒənt] Reisebüro(kaufmann/frau)
varied ['veərɪd] abwechslungreich, verschiedenartig

Your hotel room

Write the following in the correct places:

Internet access, double bed, non-smoking room, with a shower, on the ground floor, with a bath, single bed, executive suite, mini-bar, on the first floor, TV, twin beds, on the top floor.

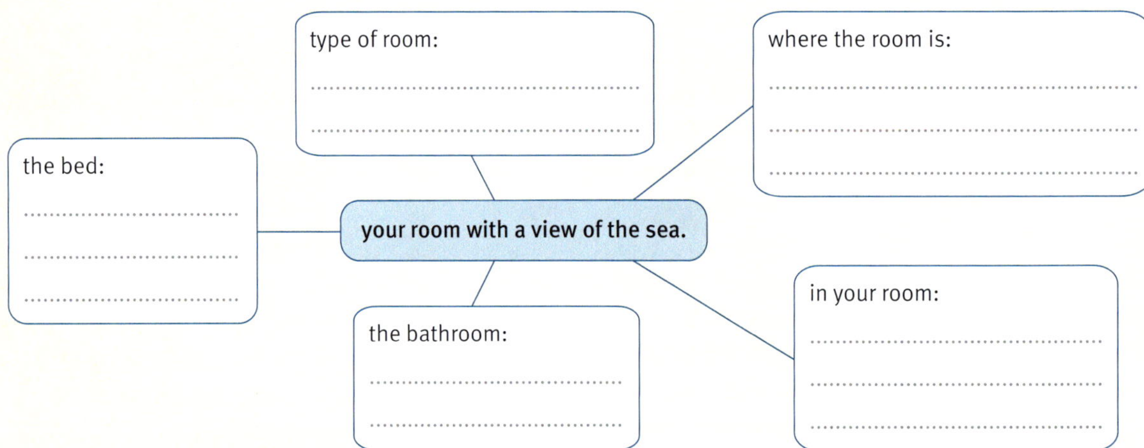

Now you can do the following things in the world of travel. You can:
✔ read and understand a hotel leaflet
✔ use some words in British English or American English
✔ answer the phone and put a caller through
✔ list your requirements for a hotel room
✔ write a holiday postcard to a friend.

Personal diary **Write about your last lesson.**

Just too much!

A 45-year-old Indian man called Kapila Pradhan, from the eastern Indian state of Orissa, left his home and family fifteen years ago. When people from his village found him, he was living in a tree – and he is still there. Why did he leave? The reason was that he was too angry to stay at home with his wife and young son anymore. And why was he so angry? The neighbours said that it was because his wife was having an affair with his younger brother, Babuan. And soon after he left the family home, his brother moved in. But Babuan always claimed that the affair didn't begin until after Kapila had left.

Kapila's tree-house, which is over seven metres above the ground, is not very far from the edge of the forest, near a village. Some villagers take him food from time to time. One villager said, "I remember when I first saw him. When I looked up into the tree he was sitting there – all alone. He said 'hello' to me when he saw me and told me a bit about his life. I can't understand how anyone can be so angry that they go away and live in a tree for so long." His mother was really sad about all this in the beginning but now she has accepted the situation.

🔊 **L 29**

Kapila Pradhan was obviously very angry.
What do you do to make yourself feel better if you feel angry about something?

Past simple ▶ PG, page 13;
Past progressive ▶ PG, page 14

Preview

Complete these sentences.
One day, Kapila found out that his wife
.... an affair with his brother.
When he found out about the affair, Kapila
.... home.
When one of the villagers looked up into the tree, Kapila .... there all alone.
When Kapila saw the villager, he ....
'hello'.

🔑 page 94

7 Feelings and reactions

1 Chat

What sort of things make you angry? How do you react when you're angry?

2 Vocabulary check: Family members

Four family members were mentioned in the text on page 53. Put these letters in the right order and write the words in the yellow boxes: b e h o r r t – e h m o r t – n o s – e f i w

Then fill in their male / female equivalents.

female:				
male:				

Look at the family tree on page 86. How many family members can you name?

3 How to say it: Talking about feelings

The most usual way to talk about feelings is to say *I am / I was* or *I feel / I felt*. The most important thing is to find the right word. In a game called *How did they feel?*, players get cards with words for feelings on them. They have to match the feelings to people's stories. Here are three of those stories. Match the feelings on these cards to the numbers in the stories.

amused ☐ annoyed ☐ delighted ☐ furious ☐

happy ☐ relieved ☐ sad ☐ shocked ☐

Story 1: Anna asked her partner to cook the dinner one evening last week because she expected to be late home. When she opened the door there he was, in front of the TV with a beer in his hand. That was not what she wanted to see. She was **(1)**. She grabbed the beer and poured it over his head. He was quite **(2)** by that actually. He just laughed and then they ordered a Chinese takeaway.

Story 2: Tom was busy at his computer yesterday when he heard a huge 'bang'. It was a gas explosion. His desk is next to the window, and he could see that there were a lot of injured people in the street and they all had very white faces. They obviously felt **(3)** by what they had seen. Everybody was very **(4)** that so many people were injured but they were **(5)** that nobody had died.

Story 3: Last Sunday evening, we were just in the middle of dinner when the phone rang. I felt a bit **(6)** because we usually have our answering machine on at dinnertime, but we'd forgotten to put it on that day. Afterwards I was really **(7)** about it. It was our daughter and she wanted to tell us that she's expecting her first baby. We were absolutely **(8)** – and we celebrated with champagne.

Now tell a partner about something that happened to you. Finish your story with: *And I felt very … .*

4 Who did it?

Work with a partner. Make a short quiz with five questions beginning with *Who* about the stories in exercise 3, e.g. *Who grabbed the beer?* Don't use *was* or *were* in your questions.

Now ask your quiz questions to another pair.

1 When Anna **opened** the door, her partner **was drinking** a beer in front of the TV.
2 When she **saw** that, Anna **grabbed** the beer and **poured** it over his head.

Which sentence tells you about
☐ a) things that happened one after the other?
☐ b) something that happened in the middle of another situation or activity?

5a What were you doing?

Answer this question:
What **was** Anna's partner **doing** when she arrived home?

He ....

Make a note of what you were doing at these specific times.
at midday yesterday   *when your teacher walked in*
at 9.30 yesterday evening   *when you heard about the*
at midnight on 31ˢᵗ December   *terrorist attacks in New York*
when it got light this morning

Now ask a partner questions with *What **were** you **doing** at
(+ a specific time) …* / *What **were** you **doing** when …* about
these moments. Were his/her answers the same as yours?

5b More questions

Work with a partner. Read the first story in exercise 3 again. Answer these questions:
What **was** Anna's partner **doing** when she grabbed his beer?

....

What **did** he **do** when she poured the beer over his head?

....

Write down two questions like these for stories 2 and 3. Ask and answer the questions together.
Compare your questions and answers with another pair.

5c ◀))) T 24 And suddenly …

Listen to the four situations. Work with a partner. Write down what the person or people were doing
when something else suddenly happened – and what they did as a result.
e.g. *She was watching a film when the television exploded. When it exploded, she screamed.*

1 *They …*   2 *He …*   3 *She …*   4 *They …*

Think about the last few days. Tell your partner two sentences about something that happened to you,
e.g. *I was having lunch in a café when my friend walked in. When she walked in I asked her to join me.*

◀))) T 25 Listen and discuss

Listen to a group of friends talking. They're grumbling about things that make them angry or annoyed.
Which places do they mention? What are the things that make them angry?

Do any of the things that the people mentioned make you annoyed, too? What else can make you angry?

Now talk about situations where you think most people would feel *nervous, disappointed, hurt,
embarrassed* or *afraid*. Have you ever felt like this?

Language study

Past simple

1 Die **einfache Vergangenheit** wird verwendet, um über einzelne (isolierte) Ereignisse in der Vergangenheit zu sprechen.

2 Sie wird ebenfalls verwendet für wiederholte Ereignisse in der Vergangenheit.

3 Und sie kann verwendet werden für ein länger andauerndes Ereignis.

4 Sie kann auch verwendet werden für eine Reihe von Ereignissen.

Match these sentences to explanations 1–4 above.

- [ ] a) *I went to that school from the age of 11 to 18.*
- [ ] b) *I went to town, then I had lunch with a friend and after that we saw a film.*
- [ ] c) *I met my future husband when I was 18.*
- [ ] d) *I visited my grandparents every Easter and Christmas. They always used to give me a present.*

Past progressive

Die **Verlaufsform in der Vergangenheit** wird verwendet, um über Handlungen zu sprechen, die sich in der Vergangenheit ereignet haben. Sie beschreibt eine Handlung als „Hintergrund" für eine andere oder zu einen bestimmten Zeitpunkt.

Write these words in the gaps: *doing, listening, watching, was, was, were.*

She .... to her favourite CD when he phoned.

What .... you .... at 10.30 yesterday evening?

I .... a film on TV.

! Den Unterschied im Gebrauch der einfachen Form der Vergangenheit und der Verlaufsform in der Vergangenheit können Sie an folgendem Satz gut erkennen:

We **were waiting** for the bus when we **saw** our old friend George.

page 94

info

Dealing with rage Road rage, air rage, any kind of rage – extreme and sudden anger is difficult to deal with. The number of air rage incidents has increased alarmingly over the years. One of the main causes of extreme anger in the air is too much alcohol and passengers are warned not to drink too much. Some airlines have now put together a few tips on what people can do if they feel that they are getting angry:

- don't get annoyed about something you cannot change
- take a few deep breaths
- look away from the thing or person who is making you angry
- close your eyes and imagine something positive and relaxing.

The results of air rage can be disastrous – people can die, planes can crash – or it can be very annoying for other passengers who are unnecessarily delayed. Perhaps, anger management therapy for some people – and no alcohol on planes – would help.

L 30

1 Grammar: Past simple and past progressive

Cross out the verbs that are **not** correct.

1 The students *were waiting / waited* when the teacher arrived. When she *was coming / came* in they *were saying / said* 'hello'. **(3 points)**
2 When Carol *was seeing / saw* her friend, he *was walking / walked* towards the station, but when she *was calling / called* his name he *was stopping / stopped* to speak to her. **(4 points)**
3 What *was she doing / did she do* when the phone rang? She *was listening / listened* to some music. And what *was she doing / did she do* when the phone rang? She *was answering / answered* it. **(4 points)**

Read this situation. Are the statements below true (T) or false (F)?

Sue was having dinner when her doorbell rang. She opened the door and saw her boyfriend, Tom. He smiled at her and gave her some flowers.

4 ☐ Sue started dinner before the doorbell rang.
5 ☐ She was in the middle of dinner when the doorbell rang.
6 ☐ She continued eating when the doorbell rang.
7 ☐ She opened the door when the doorbell rang.
8 ☐ She was opening the door when the doorbell rang.
9 ☐ Tom was smiling at her when she opened the door.
10 ☐ He was holding some flowers when she opened the door.
11 ☐ He smiled at her when she opened the door.
12 ☐ He gave her some flowers when she opened the door.

1 point for each correct answer — My score: **20**

2 How to say it: Talking about feelings

1 Put these words in the right order to ask about someone's feelings.

about – did – feel – how – that – you

.... ? **(1 point)**

2 Number these answers 1–4 from the least to the most annoyed: I felt … annoyed.

☐ a) rather ☐ c) extremely
☐ b) very ☐ d) a bit

1 point for each correct answer — My score: **5**

3 Vocabulary: Family members

Write the words for two female and two male family members in each of the generations.

	females	males
your generation		
an older generation		
a younger generation		

1/2 a point for each correct answer — My score: **6**

4 Pronunciation

Look at Story 1 in exercise 3 on page 54. Find the eight past verbs ending with *-ed*. How is the *-ed* pronounced? Write them in the correct columns:

d (like play**ed**)	t (like walk**ed**)	id (like visit**ed**)

🔊 **L 31** Listen to the story and check your answers.

1/2 a point for each correct answer — My score: **4**

5 🔊 L 32 Listening

Listen and choose one of these words to describe the people's feelings: *sad, amused, delighted, annoyed, relieved, shocked.*

1 .... 4 ....
2 .... 5 ....
3 ....

p. 95
p. 109
WWW

1 point for each correct answer — My score: **5**

Over to you
My total score: [   ] **40**

40–36 = Excellent   **35–31** = Very good   **30–26** = Good
25–21 = Okay   **20** or below = You need a bit more practice.
Look at the **Help** suggestions in the **Checkpoint**.

CHECKPOINT

How confident do you feel about what you've learnt and practised? Tick the appropriate boxes.

Grammar focus: The past *(I went …, I was going …)*	☐	☐	☐	**Help** ► Pocket Grammar, pages (13, 14) **17**
Vocabulary: Families and feelings	☐	☐	☐	► Vocabulary, page 109
How to say it: Expressing how you feel about things	☐	☐	☐	► Functions bank, page 114

Personal diary **Write about your last lesson.**

Tips for learners **Using your dictionary**

Most learners at A2 level choose to use a bilingual dictionary. Some prefer a monolingual dictionary. The important thing about dictionaries is when and how you use them.

- Make sure that you look at the introduction in your dictionary carefully. You will find a lot of useful information there about symbols that are used, abbreviations, etc.
- Don't forget that the first translation you see for a word might not be the one you want. Read through all the translations and decide which one is correct. If you aren't sure, turn to the German-English part and look up the word you've chosen in that direction – just to check.
- People don't normally use dictionaries when they are speaking. It's better to ask the other person for help. But use your dictionary when you're reading or writing.
- Don't over-use your dictionary. Always try to understand words in their context first … before you pick up your dictionary.

Before you go on to Unit 8, try to find time to do the ***Getting ready*** page.   

- talk about money and the part it plays in your life
- focus on the use of passives *(She is paid …, They were given …)*
- practise expressing obligation and ability
- review vocabulary about money and about parts of the body

What a waste!

From time to time, we can read newspaper reports about the way the government spends taxpayers' money. Many people feel that it isn't right that so much money is taken from them and that large sums of it are often spent on what *they* feel are unnecessary projects.

It is, perhaps, possible to explain why one government department spent £323 million on office furniture in eight years – even though the general public doesn't know how many offices there were to furnish! And what about the £2,700 million that were *overspent* by the Ministry of Defence in *one* year – well, we all want to feel safe, don't we? But it isn't always the *large* payments that are the most difficult to accept. Eyebrows were certainly raised …

- at the £140,000 that was spent on a study of cafés (result of the study: people don't go to cafés where the coffee isn't good)
- at the cost (£50) of changing a 35 pence light bulb in a government office
- at the cost (£77,000) of sending a team of artists to the North Pole to make a snowman
- and at the £5,000 that were paid to a Japanese artist to drink large quantities of beer and then walk along a wooden beam.

Analysts claim that enormous sums of money are wasted by the government – almost £1,400 a year for every man, woman and child in the UK. That's a lot of money! Most people would like to know more about where their money goes.

 L 33

What do you think your taxes should or shouldn't be spent on?

A Japanese artist performing for £5,000

Present passive ▶ PG, page 23; Past passive ▶ PG, page 24

Preview

Write these words in the sentences: *are, is, was, were*

A lot of taxpayers' money .... wasted every year.

Millions of pounds .... spent on defence last year.

A Japanese artist .... paid £5,000 for her project.

People .... not always told enough about where their money goes.

page 95

8 Money

1 Chat

What things would you like your government (national or local) to spend more money or less money on?

2 Vocabulary check: Parts of the body

On page 59, you read that a lot of people *raised their eyebrows* when they heard about the money that the government wasted. Does this mean **a)** they were negatively *surprised or* **b)** they were pleased? Something can cost you *an arm and a leg*. Does this mean that it was **a)** cheap *or* **b)** expensive?

Work in small groups. Write down eight more words for parts of the body as quickly as you can. The first group to finish should shout 'Stop!' Find out how many different words you've got in the class.

3 🔊 T 26 People and their money

Listen to the four short conversations about money. Write the numbers 1–4 next to the topics that the people speak about.

- ☐ earning money
- ☐ inheriting money
- ☐ investing money
- ☐ saving money
- ☐ spending money
- ☐ lending money

Which photo relates to the other two expressions? What do those expressions mean?

☐  ☐  ☐  ☐

4 Grammar focus: Present passive and past passive ▶ LS, page 62

She **isn't paid** very much in her new job, she **was paid** more per hour in her old job.
But in her old job, her travelling expenses **weren't paid**. They **are paid** now.

Which verbs tell you about things that used to / didn't use to happen? ☐ blue ☐ green
Do these sentences tell you who exactly paid / pays the money to her? ☐ yes ☐ no

4a Where do your taxes go?

Work in small groups. Talk about the facilities that are paid for out of your taxes.
E.g. *The children's playgroup is run by the local education department.*

Teachers Streets Flowers and trees The park Rubbish bins in the street Domestic rubbish	is are	cleaned emptied looked after paid (for) planted repaired collected	by our local government. by the (parks) department. every week. on (Fridays).

What else happens in your town?

things you can talk about: the local newspaper, our post, our local beer, old newspapers, the local buses, my telephone bill, the national football team, the corner shop, …	useful verbs: cleaned, collected, delivered, emptied, owned, operated by, printed, produced, run by, sent, sponsored by

You work for an insurance company. There were some break-ins in your area last weekend and some valuable things were stolen. You want to compare information with a colleague. Work with a partner. Look at page 87.

4c **What was true?**

Work in small groups. Write down six statements about the past, using the passive. Three of your statements should be true, and three should be false. Here are some examples:

The song 'Yesterday' was sung by the Rolling Stones.
The last local election was won by the ... party.
Our English books were printed in Germany.

Now read your sentences to the class.
The others should correct your false sentences,
like this:

> *No, that's not right.*
> *The song 'Yesterday' wasn't sung by the Rolling*
> *Stones, it was sung by the Beatles.*

5 **How to say it: Expressing obligation and ability**

Tick the sentences here that are true for you.

- [ ] a) I **must** save some money this year.
- [ ] b) I **have to** pay my rent next week.
- [ ] c) I **don't have to** pay my taxes next month.
- [ ] d) I **mustn't** spend too much money this weekend.
- [ ] e) I **can** afford to go out for dinner tomorrow.
- [ ] f) I **can't** afford to go on holiday this year.

Read this short text.
I must work a lot this year. Luckily, I don't have to work at weekends and so that means I can still see my friends and do some sport. I can't go out very much on weekdays, though, because I have to get up very early in the mornings.

Now read it again with a partner, and change the words 'this year' in the first sentence to 'last year'. Make all the other necessary changes. Write in the past forms of the verbs in this table.

Remember

I must = Ich muss (obligation comes from me)
I have to = Ich muss (obligation comes from another person)
I mustn't = Ich darf nicht
I don't have to = Ich muss nicht

present	past
must	
don't have to	
can	
can't	

 🔊 **T 27 Listen and discuss**

Listen to a family talking about their financial situation. The father is out of work at the moment, and the mother only works part-time – so they are a bit short of money. Which money-saving strategies do they suggest? Which do they think are good ideas, which are bad ideas?

Which of the family's ideas about saving money would be good ideas for you if you needed to live more cheaply for a while?

Now talk about the way you spend your money. Do you make a budget? Do you spend spontaneously? Or do you simply spend your money until it's all gone?

Language study

Present passive and past passive

Wie im Deutschen kann man im Englischen viele Aktivsätze ins Passiv setzen.
Active: *The pensions department **spent** a lot of money on furniture last year.*
Passive: *A lot of money **was spent** on furniture last year.*
Dieser Passivsatz sagt nichts darüber aus, wer das Geld ausgegeben hat.

Passivsätze werden mit dem Verb *to be* und dem Partizip der Vergangenheit des Hauptsverbs gebildet.
Die Form des *to be* gibt die Zeitstufe des Satzes an (Präsens, Präteritum, ...).

Complete these sentences with the correct form of *to be*:

Present passive: She .... paid every Friday. That's unusual because office employees ....
usually paid once a month.

Past passive: Our town .... voted 'Best Town Centre' last year. The flowers that ....
planted in the main square were beautiful.

In Passivsätzen *kann* man auch etwas darüber aussagen, wer eine Handlung ausgeführt hat, indem
man das Wort *by* benutzt.
*The 'Best Town Centre' prize of £5,000 was presented to the people of the town **by James Jordan from
the BBC.***
Eine Information dieser Art steht am Ende des Satzes.

Sie können das Passiv auch in anderen Zeiten verwenden, z. B.:

1 *The outside of the town hall **is being cleaned** this week.*
2 *Work on the main entrance **has** already **been started**.*
3 *When I walked past there yesterday, the main door **was being painted**.*

page 95

Money and the Internet Cheques, credit and debit cards have all replaced cash as
ways of paying in shops. Credit cards are easy to use but are dangerous for some people who
spend more than they have. They then find themselves in debt and have
to pay very high interest to the credit
card companies.

Nowadays, a lot of people buy on the
Internet. Just 'click here' and that's it.
Spending money on the Internet is easy
and anonymous – and this can make it
rather risky. But the Internet can also be
used to *earn* money. In America, 72% of
all households are thinking about starting
a business from home – and the Internet
features in the majority of their ideas. So
you can spend money and earn money on
the Internet, and more and more people
are now managing their money on the
Internet by using Internet banking services.

L 34

1 Grammar: Passives

Complete these sentences with the correct passive form (present or past) of the verbs given: *clean, design, discover, drink, print, sing, spend, write.*

1 Othello .... by Shakespeare.

2 The streets .... every Tuesday.

3 A lot of beer .... after the final.

4 .... our books .... in Germany?

5 *Yesterday* .... by the Beatles.

6 We saw some buildings that .... by Gaudi.

7 Penicillin .... In 1928.

8 Millions .... on defence every year.

| **1** point for each correct word | My score: | **16** |

2 L 35 Listening

Where do these five conversations about money take place? Number the correct places 1–5.

- [ ] in a bank
- [ ] at a breakfast table
- [ ] at a station
- [ ] in a newsagent's
- [ ] in a restaurant
- [ ] in a coin dealer's shop

L 36 Listen again. Which conversation is about …

a) [ ] paying a bill?
b) [ ] getting some change?
c) [ ] pocket money?

| **1** point for each correct answer | My score: | **8** |

3 How to say it: Expressing obligation and ability

Which is the correct way to express an obligation or ability? Cross out the wrong words.

1 I *mustn't / don't have to* buy my food at the supermarket.
2 I can't *Chinese / speak Chinese.*
3 I *mustn't / don't have to* block the hospital entrance.
4 I can *swim / to swim.*

| **1** point for each correct answer | My score: | **4** |

4 Pronunciation

Underline the word in which the letters in **bold** sound different.

1 b**u**lb   p**u**blic   q**u**antity
2 **a**rtist   dep**a**rtment   unnecess**a**ry
3 **c**ertainly   **c**laim   ex**c**lain
4 govern**m**ent   **m**oney   pro**j**ect
5 eyebr**ow**   h**ow**   kn**ow**

L 37 Listen and check your answers.

| **1** point for each correct answer | My score: | **5** |

5 Vocabulary: Money

Name seven things that you can do with money. I can …

1 e _ _ _ _ some when I work.

2 i _ _ _ _ _ _ _ _ some from an aunt.

3 i _ _ _ _ _ _ _ some in a business.

4 l _ _ _ _ some to a friend.

5 s _ _ _ _ some in my bank account.

6 s _ _ _ _ _ some on new clothes.

7 w _ _ _ _ _ some on stupid things.

| **1** point for each correct answer | My score: | **7** |

p. 95

p. 110

WWW

Over to you
My total score: [ ] **40**

40–36 = Excellent   **35–31** = Very good   **30–26** = Good
25–21 = Okay   **20** or below = You need a bit more practice.
Look at the **Help** suggestions in the **Checkpoint**.

CHECKPOINT

How confident do you feel about what you've learnt and practised? Tick the appropriate boxes.

Help

Grammar focus: Present passive (*She is paid ...*) and past passive (*They were given ...*)
▶ Pocket Grammar, pages (23, 24) **25**

Vocabulary: Money
▶ Vocabulary, page 110

How to say it: Expressing obligation and ability
▶ Functions bank, page 115

Personal diary Write about your last lesson.

Tips for learners Practising speaking

You get a lot of opportunities to speak English during your lesson – but what about when you are outside the classroom? Here are some ideas about how you can practise:

- You could form a group (of people in your class and others, too) which can meet regularly and speak English together. It would be a good idea to agree on a topic in advance. If you don't do this, it may be difficult to get started.
- You could record yourself and then listen carefully to how you sound, or exchange recordings with someone else.
- You could try to find an English-speaker in your town. Perhaps you could meet and speak English for half an hour and then German for half an hour.
- Talk to yourself in English while you are cooking, doing the housework or are out for a ride on your bike.
- Take every opportunity you can to speak English!

Before you go on to Unit 9, try to find time to do the *Getting ready* page.

In this unit, you're going to ...

- talk about traditions and festivals in different countries
- focus on possible future events (*If we go to London, we'll / we might / we could ...*), and planned events (*They'll be here tomorrow.*)
- practise expressing probability and possibility (*probably, might*)
- review vocabulary of numbers, days, months and times

A special festival

Dear Kate,

Time has flown by since Don and I moved to Zurich, hasn't it? I really hope you can come and visit us soon. There's a special festival here on the third weekend in April – so please come then! The festival's called Sechseläuten – which means 'ringing 6 o'clock' ... and this is to mark the end of winter.

If you get here before noon on the Sunday, you'll be in time to see the children's parade in the afternoon – lots of kids in historical costumes. Then on the Monday afternoon there'll be another parade through the streets. At 6 o'clock the church bells ring and members of the guilds (all men!) will ride around a huge bonfire on horseback. There's a sort of a snowman on the top – with fireworks in his head! They say that if the head explodes quickly, the summer will be long and hot. They've done this since the 19th century. I can't remember how long it took last year – but it was great to see – I'm enclosing a photo of what you'll see if you get here on or before the Monday. Well – will you come? Now, I'll just tell you a bit more about our new flat – we're very pleased with it.

 L 38

Which festival or special day would you choose to invite people from another country to?

Future simple ▶ PG, page 18; First conditional ▶ PG, page 28

Preview

When will the children's parade take place? It'll take place on ....

When will the snowman burn? It'll burn on ....

Cross out the wrong verb:

If Kate arrives on Monday, *she'll see / she won't see* the children's parade.

If she arrives on Monday morning, *she'll be / she won't be* in time to see the bonfire.

page 95

9 Things people do

1 Chat

What was the last public holiday or special celebration for you? What did you do on that day?

2 The end of winter

Read the letter on page 65. Pay special attention to the information on the left:

Zurich	Annapolis, near Washington DC
Sechseläuten	
3rd weekend in April	
members of the guilds	
huge bonfire	
snowman	
19th century	

T 28 Now listen to a man who phoned a radio show about another celebration of the end of winter. Write down the parallel information in the column on the right.

3 Vocabulary check: Numbers, days, months and ti

When is the Sechseläuten festival in Zurich?
Take turns, going round the class, saying an ordinal number, like this

Now check that you can remember the days of the week and the mon
What's the 4th month? What's the 7th day?

What time do the church bells ring at Sechseläuten?
Now work in groups of four. Say all these times (*not* with the 24-hour system).
18.00   18.30   18.15   18.45   18.25   18.35   12.00   24.00

4 How to say it: Expressing probability and possibility

Will you be at the meeting? Number these sentences 1–5 (1= the most probable, 5 = the least probable).

☐ I **might be** at the meeting.
☐ I **won't be** at the meeting.
☐ I **probably won't be** at the meeting.
☐ I **'ll be** at the meeting.
☐ I **'ll probably be** at the meeting.

Use these five expressions to tell a partner about your whereabouts at different times next weekend.

5 Grammar focus: Future simple and first conditional ▶ LS, page 68

Will Kate **see** the children's parade?
She**'ll see** it if she **gets** to Zurich before noon on Sunday.
If **she's** late, she**'ll have to** watch it on TV in the evening.

Your English course **will finish** soon.
Will you **have** time to do another course when this one **finishes**?
Yes, I think I**'ll be able** to do another course when this one **finishes**.

 ## What will you do if ...?

What will you do if the following things happen next week? *You win the lottery, it rains all the time, your boss gives you three days off, you can't come to the lesson, you don't understand something in the 'Over to you' section.*

Work with a partner. Ask and answer questions beginning with *What will you do if ...?*

 ## They became rich

This couple inherited a lot of money from a distant relative a few years ago. They now have a *very* extravagant lifestyle. Write down two more things that you can add to this list.

- They drink champagne every day.
- They play golf at a very exclusive club.
- They live in a big house in the country.
- They go to the theatre or opera every week.
- They always travel first class.

Unfortunately, the man has started gambling. He has now lost most of their money, but his wife doesn't know. He plans to go to the casino on Saturday and try to win back as much as he can. But how will their lifestyle be different if he loses everything?

Discuss this in groups. Start your suggestions with *If he loses all their money, they won't be able to / they will have to ... .*

Remember

the future of **must** = **will have to**
the future of **can** = **will be able to**

 ## What will the consequences be?

If Kate arrives in Zurich on Sunday evening, she'll see the Sechseläuten bonfire on Monday, but she won't be able to watch the children's parade.

Work with a partner. Think of one positive and one negative consequence of these things that might happen in the future:
If they build a new shopping centre outside our town ..., If it snows at the weekend ..., If I get a full-time job ..., If our local post office closes down ..., If my neighbours move to Spain ..., If ... .

 ## ◁)) T 29 Listen and discuss

Listen to the radio presenter on the phone-in show. He wants people to contact him with interesting stories. What sort of stories is he interested in?

You're thinking about going to Australia for Christmas next year. If you go there, how will your Christmas be different from a Christmas at home?

Now go on to talk about any other celebrations or festivals that you know about – from anywhere in the world.

Language study

Future simple (future with *will*)

1 Die Zukunft mit *will* wird verwendet, um über Tatsachen und geplante Ereignisse zu sprechen.
2 Sie wird auch verwendet, um über spontane Entscheidungen zu sprechen.
3 Man kann die Zukunft mit *will* auch verwenden, um über etwas Vermutungen anzustellen.

Match these sentences to explanations 1–3 above:

☐ a) *I'll see you near the bonfire then.*
☐ b) *I think there'll be a lot of people there.*
☐ c) *The main Sechseläuten parade will be on Monday.*

Beachten Sie bitte: Die Form bleibt für alle Personen gleich: *will* (positiv), *won't* (negativ). *Will* wird fast immer zu *'ll* verkürzt.

Future simple of must and can

present	future
I must (+ verb) …	I'll have to (+ verb) …
I don't have to (+ verb) …	I won't have to (+ verb) …
I can (+ verb) …	I'll be able to (+ verb) …
I can't (+ verb) …	I won't be able to (+ verb) …

First conditional

Der Bedingungssatz Typ 1 wird gebildet aus der **einfachen Vergangenheit** im *if*-Satz und der **Zukunft** im Hauptsatz.

Write these words in the sentences: *be, come, don't, is, miss, will, won't.*

I .... at the next lesson if my meeting .... a long one.

If I .... to my English class next week, I .... Unit 10!

 Verwenden Sie nie *will* im *if*-Satz. **Remember:** If + will makes teachers ill!

page 95

---

info

When is the New Year? Europe celebrates the New Year at midnight on 31st December, but many people around the world (and some in Europe) celebrate it at other times. The Chinese New Year is celebrated at a new moon between 21st January and 21st February – with colourful street parades and fireworks. The Thai New Year is celebrated between 13th and 15th April – by throwing water. The Islamic New Year moves all the time – about eleven days earlier on the Gregorian calendar each year. It is possible for Muslims to have two New Year celebrations in one year – like in 2008. India has many New Years – in the Sikh calendar it is celebrated on March 14th, in the Punjab on April 13th and in the Gujarat in November, two days after Diwali, the Hindu festival of lights. Travel around the world you can celebrate the New Year again and again!

 L 39

1 Grammar: Future simple and first conditional

Write the missing words in the gaps.

1 Next year, I .... be in Washington in March. I hope I .... be .... to see the burning of the socks.

2 If I .... there on the right day, I .... certainly .... some photos of it.

3 I'm sure my friends .... believe me if I come back home and .... have any photos to show them!

4 I .... take some old socks with me (I'm not sure about that yet), so that I .... be the only one with nothing to burn!

5 If I'm .... there on the right day, I'll .... to show them a newspaper photo instead.

1 point for each correct word | My score: **12**

2 Pronunciation

What sound does the letter **c** make in these words? Write them in the correct columns.
since, historical, costumes, special, celebration, country, century

a **k** sound	an **s** sound	a **sh** sound

L 40 Listen and check your answers.

1 point for each correct answer | My score: **7**

3 **L 41** Listening

Christmas is different in different parts of the world. Are the people you hear taking about Christmas down under or Christmas in Europe? Write the numbers on the lines.

Down under: ....

In Europe: ....

1 point for each correct answer | My score: **8**

4 Vocabulary: Days and months

Write the name of these days and months. (Monday = the first day of the week.)

1 1st month ....
2 2nd day ....
3 3rd day ....
4 4th day ....
5 5th day ....
6 6th day ....
7 7th month ....

1 point for each correct answer | My score: **7**

5 How to say it: Expressing probability

How certain is it? Which two are 100% certain, which two are 90% certain and which two are only 50% certain?

1 I'll be there. ....%
2 I might be there. ....%
3 I'll probably be there. ....%
4 I won't be there. ....%
5 Perhaps I'll be there. ....%
6 I probably won't be there. ....%

1 point for each correct answer | My score: **6**

p. 95

p. 111

▶ WWW

> **Over to you**
> My total score: ☐ **40**
>
> **40–36** = Excellent   **35–31** = Very good   **30–26** = Good
> **25–21** = Okay   **20** or below = You need a bit more practice.
> Look at the **Help** suggestions in the **Checkpoint**.

CHECKPOINT

How confident do you feel about what you've learnt and practised? Tick the appropriate boxes.

Help

Grammar focus: Possible future events
(*If we go to London, we'll / we might / we could …*), and planned events (*They'll be here tomorrow.*)
☐ ☐ ☐
▶ Pocket Grammar, pages (18, 28) **29**

Vocabulary: Numbers, days, months and times
☐ ☐ ☐
▶ Vocabulary, page 111

How to say it: Expressing probability and possibility (*probably, might*)
☐ ☐ ☐
▶ Functions bank, page 115

Personal diary Write about your last lesson.

Tips for learners Practising reading

There are some golden rules for reading texts – in the classroom and outside.
- Read the text quite quickly to get a general idea of what it is about – don't worry about the words you don't know, unless an unknown word is the key word of the text.
- Then read it again more slowly and focus on the details of the text that you want to focus on or the details that you need to focus on in order to do a task.
- Don't follow each word that you read with your finger – that's too slow.
- And don't stop too often to look up a word in the dictionary.
- Clues from other components of the text can often help you. Is there a headline or title? Is there a picture?
- Read as many different sorts of texts as you can – in addition to the texts in this book, you could read newspapers and magazines (not too 'serious'). You could also read English on the Internet. Try looking at www.bbc.co.uk where you can read about the news from all over the world. Last but not least, read the English on the packets of things that you buy.

Before you go on to Unit 10, try to find time to do the *Getting ready* page.   

▶ In this unit, you're going to ...

- talk about future
- focus on speaking about the future using *I'm going to ...* and several other verb forms that you already know
- practise talking about wishes, hopes and dreams
- review vocabulary about the media and the news

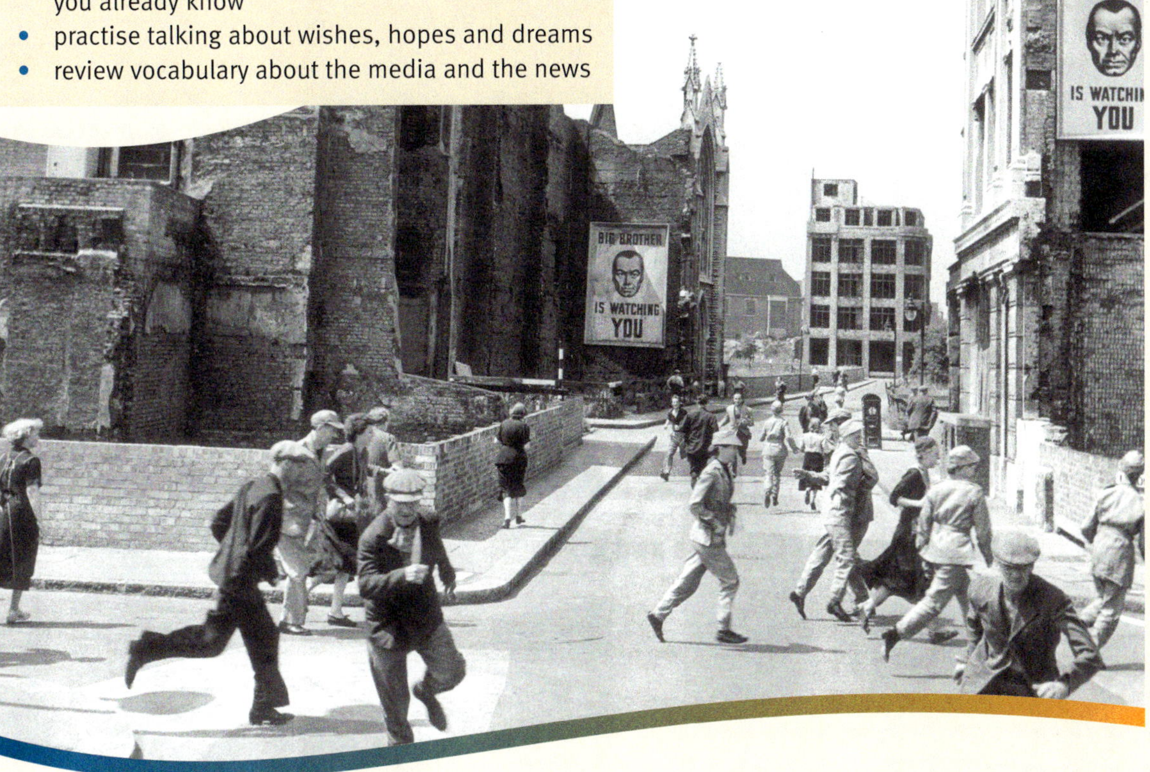

Looking into the future

Looking into the future can be scary. In 1938, a radio play by Orson Welles caused panic across America. The play included realistic news bulletins that announced the arrival of aliens from Mars. Many people didn't realise that these bulletins were part of the play – and they feared for their future. But aliens have never landed ... that vision of the future has not come true.

In 1949, a book entitled *Nineteen Eighty-Four* by George Orwell was published. At the time, 1984 seemed a long time away. His vision was of a totalitarian society in which everybody is controlled by the state and where nobody is allowed to be an 'individual'. The expression 'Big Brother is watching you!' is often quoted nowadays when people speak about things like security camera systems or biometric passports.

Do we really want to know what is going to happen in the future? It's certainly good to have warnings about earthquakes and hurricanes, and most people would probably like to know if any big change is going to happen in their work, home, financial or family situation. But do people really want to know what is going to happen in their lives – in every detail? 🔊 **L 42**

What about you? How much would you like to know about your future now?

Preview	*going to* future ▶ PG, page 19

Are 1–6 about the present or the future? Write P or F in the boxes.

1. ☐ They're going to read *Nineteen Eighty-Four* in their next course.
2. ☐ What's she doing?
3. ☐ 'Big Brother' isn't watching us.
4. ☐ What's he going to do about it?
5. ☐ I'm reading something else at the moment.
6. ☐ They aren't going to put a security camera in the sauna! 🔑 **page 95**

10 Sometime in the future

1 Chat

What do you know about the ways in which people try to look into the future? Have you ever tried to do this?

2 How to say it: Wishes, hopes and dreams

Match the two parts of these sentences.

1 **I'd love to**
2 **I hope I'll be**
3 **My dream future would be**
4 **All I want**

a) is to stay healthy in the future.
b) to buy a motorbike and ride across America.
c) move to Spain when I retire.
d) able to have a long holiday next year.

Talk to a partner. Tell your partner about your ideas, dreams and hopes for your future. Use the expressions above.

3 Grammar focus: The future ▶ LS, page 74

In Unit 9, you used these two ways of talking about the future:

1 If we **leave** here at 6 o'clock, we**'ll catch** the 18.30 train.
2 Okay, I**'ll phone** my friends and tell them, and they**'ll** probably **meet** us at the station.

Here are three more:

3 Our train **arrives** in London at 20.15.
4 We**'re having** dinner with my friends in a new Indian restaurant.
5 And on Saturday we**'re going to be** tourists in London.

3a Which future?

Work with a partner. Read the sentences in the *Grammar focus* above and match them to these five descriptions.

Sentence ☐ has a spontaneous suggestion / decision or fact about the future in it.

Sentence ☐ is about something that will only happen if something else happens first.

Sentence ☐ is about a general / personal plan or intention.

Sentence ☐ is about information from a timetable or schedule.

Sentence ☐ is about an arrangement that has been made.

How would you say the sentences in the *Grammar focus* in German?

3b 🔊 T 30 Performing this weekend

Listen to the local radio news. Write the missing verbs in the newsreader's text.

This weekend, Southend Players (1) .... a play by Oscar Wilde at the Dome. The play is called *The Importance of Being Earnest*. It (2) .... at 7.30 and if you (3a) .... the ticket office later today, they (3b) .... a ticket for you. Our reporter (4) .... the play on Friday and he (5) .... here in the studio on Saturday morning to tell you what he thought about it. Well, that's something to look forward to, isn't it?

Now work with a partner and match the verbs you have written to the explanations about future tenses in the *Grammar focus*.

1 ....   2 ....   3a + 3b ....

4 ....   5 ....

Question tags (like the *isn't it*? at the end of the text) make a sentence into a question. The rule is: positive sentence ▶ negative question tag / negative sentence ▶ positive question tag.

3c What are your intentions / plans?

Tell a partner about something that you are going to do:

after this lesson   *tomorrow*   *on Saturday*   *in the summer*   *when you retire*

Your intentions can also be very immediate. For example, if you have a car key in your hand and you're walking towards a car, we could say: *You're going to open the car and drive away.*

Work with your partner and think up two descriptions (like the one above with the car key) – one description each. When everybody is ready, tell the rest of the class your description, beginning: *I … .* The others can guess what you're going to do: *Are you going to … ?*

4 Vocabulary check: Getting news and information

Where can you find out about things that are going to happen in your town or village. Complete these words with the missing vowels:

on	t _ l _ v _ s _ _ _ n	**in**	m _ g _ z _ n _ s
	the r _ d _ _ _		n _ w s p _ p _ r s
	the _ n t _ r n _ t	**from**	f r _ _ _ n d s
	n _ t _ c _ b _ _ _ r d s		n _ _ g h b _ _ _ r s
	p _ s t _ r s		c _ l l _ _ g _ _ _ s

What *is* going to happen in the near future in your town or village? How did you hear about it?

🔊 T 31 Listen and discuss

Listen to a group of students who have just finished their English course. What are they talking about?

What was the main difference between their learning situation and yours?

Look at page 88. You'll find a list of the things these students spoke about. Now you can talk about how you are going to continue with your English.

Language study

The future

Sie kennen verschiedene Möglichkeiten, um über die **Zukunft** zu sprechen.

Aus Unit 9:

1 Sie können die **Zukunft mit** *will* verwenden, um a) über Tatsachen zu sprechen, b) spontane Entscheidungen zu treffen oder c) Vermutungen zu äußern.
a) *I'll be* at the next lesson. b) *I'll bring* the wine. c) *I think the party* **will be** *really good fun.*

2 Sie können *if*-**Sätze vom Typ 1** verwenden, um über die Folgen von etwas zu sprechen, das in der Zukunft geschehen oder könnte.
If it **rains** *on Saturday, we* **won't go** *for a picnic, we'll go to the cinema instead.*

Und aus dieser Unit:

3 Sie können die **einfache Gegenwart** verwenden mit Bezug auf Fahr- und Zeitpläne eher offizieller Art.
My train **leaves** *at six o'clock.*

4 Sie können die **Verlaufsform der Gegenwart** verwenden, um über feste Vereinbarungen zu sprechen.
We're going to the theatre on Saturday. (the tickets have already been bought)

5 Sie können die **Zukunft mit** *going to* verwenden, um über Pläne und Absichten zu sprechen.
I'm going to stay at home tomorrow evening.

6 Sie können auch die Wahrscheinlichkeit, dass etwas passieren wird, ausdrücken:
I might be here next week. / I'll **probably** *be here next week. /* **Perhaps** *I'll be here next week.*

---

info

What will be successful in the future?

People who invent or create something new need to be able to see into the future and recognise what will be a success. The inventors of TV did this, even though in the early days people asked 'who on earth will want to sit at home and watch pictures in a box?' Twelve publishers didn't 'see and recognise' when they rejected J.K. Rowling's manuscript of the first Harry Potter book. By 2005 she was the 9th richest woman in the UK!

Nobody ever dreamed that mobile phones would be able to receive e-mails and TV or that computers would become such a central part of our lives.

This is what you should do if you have a great idea for the future:
a) don't tell too many people about it (or should that be – don't tell *anybody*?)
b) contact the patent office and register your idea
c) don't give up!

 L 43

1 Grammar: The future

A friend of yours is going on holiday next week. Write the correct future forms in the gaps. Use the verbs in brackets.

1 *(go)* Where .... you ....?

2 *(be)* How long .... you .... away?

3 *(leave)* When .... your train ....

4 *(send / find)* .... you .... me a postcard if you .... a nice one?

5 *(meet)* I .... you at the station when you come back.

6 *(stay)* .... you .... to .... in a hotel?

7 *(phone)* If I miss you too much, I .... you (I'm not really sure about that though!)

> **1** point for each correct word   My score: **16**

2 L 44 Listening

A family is taking their grandma to London to celebrate her birthday next Saturday. Listen to five things that they said. What were they talking about? Write the numbers 1–5:

☐ a) a schedule or timetable
☐ b) an arrangement that is fixed and booked
☐ c) a plan or idea with nothing fixed
☐ d) a plan that depends on something else
☐ e) an offer

> **1** point for each correct answer   My score: **5**

3 Vocabulary: Getting news

You know about something that is going to happen in your town in the near future. How did you hear about it?

1 I read about it   in a   n............................... .

                 in a   m............................... .

                 on a   p............................... .

                 on the   l............................... .

2 I heard about it on the   r............................... .

                 from a   f............................... .

                 from a   n............................... .

3 I saw a report   on   t............................... .

> **1** point for each correct answer   My score: **8**

4 L 45 Pronunciation

In exercise 3b on page 73, you saw this: *Well, that's something to look forward to, isn't it?* The intonation is important. If the question tag goes up at the end, it's a genuine question and you don't know what the answer will be. If the question tag goes down, you are sure that the other person has the same opinion as you. Listen and decide if answers are expected or not.

1 (yes)   no   6 yes   no

2 yes   (no)   7 yes   no

3 yes   no   8 yes   no

4 yes   no   9 yes   no

5 yes   no

> **1** point for each correct answer   My score: **7**

5 How to say it: Wishes, hopes and dreams

Write *dream, hope, love, want* in the gaps.

1 I .... I'll be able to come to the next course.

2 I'd .... to move to France when I retire.

3 All I .... is to be near my grandchildren when I'm older.

4 My .... is to travel around the world.

> **1** point for each correct answer   My score: **4**

p. 95

p. 112

WWW

TYS, p. 83

Over to you
My total score: **40**

40–36 = Excellent   **35–31** = Very good   **30–26** = Good
25–21 = Okay   **20 or below** = You need a bit more practice.
Look at the **Help** suggestions in the **Checkpoint**.

CHECKPOINT

How confident do you feel about what you've learnt and practised? Tick the appropriate boxes.

Help

Grammar focus: The future with *I'm going to ...* and several other verb forms
- ► Pocket Grammar, pages (19) **22**

Vocabulary: The media and the news
- ► Vocabulary, page 112

How to say it: Wishes, hopes and dreams
- ► Functions bank, page 115

Personal diary   Write about your last lesson.

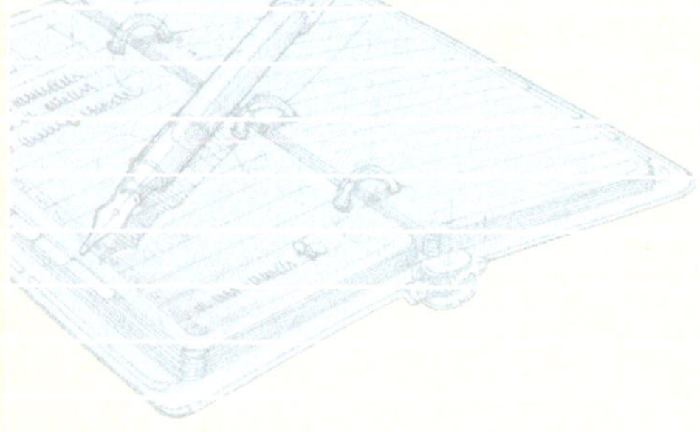

Tips for learners   Practising writing

You have probably noticed that you have done more listening, speaking and reading than writing in this course. That's because when you come for a lesson with other people, you don't *really* want to sit in the classroom quietly writing, do you?

If you would like to write a bit more, first of all, make sure that you have done all the writing tasks on the *Vocabulary* pages.

After finishing *English Network Refresher A2*, you could:
- write a private diary in English
- try writing a story for someone else to read
- choose a photo from your newspaper and write a short text to go with it
- exchange e-mails with someone in your class, telling them about your everyday life and opinions on things that are important to you.

If you write more, your writing will become more fluent – just like your speaking.

The world of words

Now it's time to play with English.

1 A word puzzle

Do this crossword puzzle. All of the words come from the text about Wakamaru on page 21.

1 Mitsubishi is a ~ company.
2 Wakamaru is about 1 metre ~ .
3 + 12 Wakamaru can ~ your carpet and ~ for you.
4 + 10 Would you spend a lot of ~ on a ~ like Wakaramu?
5 + 16 Wakamaru ~ less than 30 ~ .
6 Wakamaru can be a friend or ~ .
7 Wakamaru always agrees with you, it never ~ .
8 It moves around on ~ .

9 + 13 Would you buy a robot ~ you had ~ money ?
10 *see number 4*
11 It can ~ its own batteries.
12 *see number 3*
13 *see number 9*
14 Wakaramu runs on ~ .
15 It can also work outside and do the ~ for you.
16 *see number 5*

What are the words in the grey boxes? ....

2 Jumbled sentences

Put these words in the right order to make sentences about Wakamaru, the robot on page 21.

1 is   robot.   Mitsubish's   Wakamaru   new

....

2 clean   windows.   It   carpets   and   can

....

If there is no capital letter on the first word and no full stop after the last word, the jumbled sentence is more difficult to solve.

3 people   prefer   butler   most   have   to   would   a

....

4 robot   around   wheels   the   on   moves

....

3 A quiz

Read the article on page 15 and then answer these quiz questions about Mike Theiss.

1 How old was Mike Theiss when he first became interested in the weather?
2 Which American state did he live in when he was young?
3 Where did he stand or sit when he wanted to watch a storm?
4 What did he like listening to when there was a storm?
5 What did he like watching when there was a storm?
6 How long has he been a hurricane chaser?
7 What do most people do when a hurricane is on its way?
8 What does Mike do when a hurricane is coming?
9 What does Mike do when he gets close to the eye of a hurricane?
10 His job is exciting but it can also be ~ .

4 Word boxes

Match the words in box A with the words in box B. All the words and expressions come from the text about Mike Theiss on page 15.

A	B
dangerous	chaser
drive	equipment
eye	lightning
hurricane	of the hurricane
leave	personal things
listen to	photos
pack	thunder
photography	towards the hurricane
take	town
watch	work

5 Rhyming words

Rhyming words are words that sound the same,
e.g. *rhyme* and *time*.
Find words in the article about bullfighting (page 43) that
rhyme with these words:

1 stand ....
2 tall ....
3 name ....
4 bought ....

5 new ....
6 ground ....
7 days........................
8 blue ....

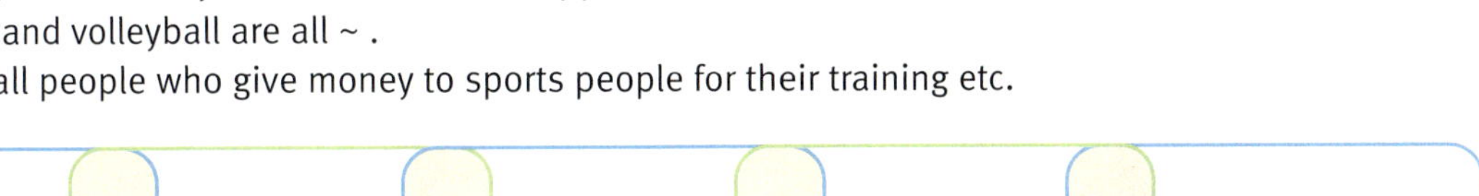

6 Word chain

Write the answers to these questions in the word chain.
The last letter of a word is the first letter of the next
word – like this:

B U L L （S） P A I N

The words all come from the text about Spain on page 43.

1 Which sport used to be very popular in Spain?
2 What's the word for your children's children?
3 Which TV programme tells you about what has happened during the day?
4 Rugby, tennis and volleyball are all ~ .
5 What do we call people who give money to sports people for their training etc.

Make your own puzzles!

Work in groups of 3 or 4. Make a puzzle like one of the puzzles in this Extra. Every puzzle should be
about one of the texts on a *Getting ready* page of units 1–10. Some tips:

1 **A word puzzle:** Choose the word or words that you want to have in the grey boxes in the end. You
can make your puzzle shorter than the one you did in this Extra.

2 **Jumbled sentences:** Make a mixture of easier and more difficult ones.

3 **A quiz:** 6 or 8 questions would also be enough.

4 **Word boxes:** You can probably find 10 examples, too.

5 **Rhyming words:** Don't worry if some of the words look and sound the same, and others only sound
the same – but look different.

6 **Word chain:** This one is rather difficult. If you can get more than 5 words, that's really good.

When you are ready, find another group that has finished and exchange puzzles. Do their puzzle.
Then exchange with another group.

In Extra C you played around with words. Now you can find out how good you are at numbers!
Write down or choose how you think you would say these numbers.

cardinal numbers[1]:   8 ....   14 ....   31 ....

106 ....

1,370 ....

ordinal numbers: 1st ....   2nd ....   3rd ....

4th ....   5th ....   12th ....

dates[2]:   22.2 ....

18.3 ....

years: 1999 ....

2006 ....

telephone numbers: 409683   ☐ forty   ninety-six   eighty-three
☐ four   oh   nine   six   eight   three

366720   ☐ three   double   six   seven   two   oh
☐ three   six   six   seven   two   nil

fractions: 1/2 ....   1/4 ....

1/3 ....   2/100 ....

decimals[3]:   2.3 ....   5.1 ....

percentages: 20 % ....

temperatures[4]:   5°C ....   −2°C ....

60°F ....

[1] Note that numbers over 999 have a comma on the line.
[2] Note than the British write dates like this: 22.11.2006. Americans would write this date: 11.22.2006.
[3] Note that you have to write a full stop in decimal numbers in English (not a comma).
[4] Note: C = Celsius, F = Fahrenheit

Personal diary **Write about your last lesson.**

p. 96

These exercises are modelled on the types of exercises in *The European Language Certificate* (TELC) examination for the A2 level.

Reading

1 Read these five texts from a newspaper carefully.

1 ☐ Our local team, The Lions, did very well on Saturday. They played their best and managed to reach the semi-finals. Unfortunately, they didn't reach the finals, but they won the B final and so they finished in 3rd place.

2 ☐ *The Jazz Open Air will take place again in the third week of August. This year's programme will be the best ever, with several internationally-known musicians coming to play as well as local musicians. You can buy tickets from the beginning of August at* www.jazzopen.co.uk.

3 ☐ The church garden party, that was held last Saturday, raised over £1,500 for the Marretti Children's Home. The manager of the home was very happy to receive the money and said that it would be spent on a new outdoor play area for the children.

4 ☐ We were all very sad to hear that Mr James Stokes, our Member of Parliament, died last week. He did a wonderful job and unfortunately couldn't realise his plans for training courses for the unemployed before his sudden death, following a car accident.

5 ☐ On Saturday evening, three young men attacked a woman who was working in the all-night shop in Station Road. They stole all the cash she had and also a large number of DVDs and CDs. Luckily Ms Davis was not injured, but she was very shocked and had to stay in hospital for one night.

Now read the newspaper headlines a)–j). Choose the best headline for each text and write the letters in the boxes.

a) **Lions in the finals**
b) **Jazz, jazz and more jazz**
c) **Congratulations boys!**
d) **Jazz in the opera house**
e) **Three young men injure shop assistant in attack**
f) **Church raises money for children's home**
g) **MP plans courses**
h) **Attack shock for all-night shop assistant**
i) **Tragic accident kills MP**
j) **Church raises money for church fund**

2 Read the texts again and complete sentences 1–5 with a), b) or c). Write the letter on the line.

1 The Lions .... a) reached the final, b) reached the semifinal and lost it, c) reached the semi-final and won it.

2 The Jazz Open Air is .... a) at the beginning of August, b) in August, c) at the end of August.

3 The Church garden party raised .... a) more than £1,500, b) less than £1,500, c) £1,500 exactly.

4 James Stokes .... a) retired from his job, b) found a new job, c) had an accident and died.

5 The three young men .... a) knew Ms Davis, b) stole only cash, c) stole cash and things they could easily sell.

☐ out of **10**

Listening

1 🔊 **L 46** You are going to hear five people speaking. Listen and decide if the statements 1–5 are true (✔) or not true (✘).

1 ☐ The speaker works five days a week.
2 ☐ The six mothers spend all their time with their children or working at home.
3 ☐ Writing is the speaker's main professional interest.
4 ☐ The speaker has an office job.
5 ☐ The speaker wouldn't like to have a 9 to 5 job in one place.

☐ out of **10**

2 🔊 **L 47** Listen again and decide if the statements are true (✔) or not true (✘).

1 ☐ The speaker leaves her house at 7.30 in the morning on the days when she goes to work.
2 ☐ The six mothers have got nine children between them.
3 ☐ The speaker has been working on his stories for about four months.
4 ☐ The weather is warmer now than it was last week.
5 ☐ The speaker lives in the north of England.

Language elements

1 Read the following e-mail and decide which word is missing. Write a)–o) in the gaps.

a) a lot of, b) about, c) been, d) do, e) does, f) for, g) friendlier, h) have, i) of, j) on, k) some, l) than, m) to, n) working, o) you

Dear Josie,

It was so nice to hear from .... again. Where .... you live now? How long .... you been living there? And what .... a job? Are you still .... at the old people's home? Sorry, ... questions! Well, let *me* tell *you* .... news. I've .... working as (1) <u>a hotel receptionist</u> (2) .... <u>two years now</u>. I started there .... my 25th birthday. It's great. It's a 4-star hotel (3) <u>in the centre</u> .... London. It's much more interesting .... my last job. I like the boss (4) <u>because she's much</u> .... <u>than the last one!</u> Where .... Tom work? Anyway, that's all for now. Please write again soon. Hope .... see you in the not-too-distant future. Don't forget, I live (5) <u>right in the centre of London</u>.

Come and visit!

Lots of love,
Amy

2 Write the questions that give the underlined information about Amy as answers.

(1) ....

(2) ....

(3) ....

(4) ....

(5) ....

☐ out of **20**

🔑 p. 96

My result: ☐ out of **40**

These exercises are modelled on the types of exercises in *The European Language Certificate* (TELC) examination for the A2 level.

Reading

1 Read the text and answer the questions below.

Planning a holiday is never a very easy thing to do – and (1) <u>it</u> gets more difficult if there are several people who are going on (2) <u>it</u> together! The problem is that people have very different ideas about what they would like to do when they're on holiday.

The first thing to decide is when. When can you take time off work? Would you like a typical winter holiday or summer holiday? Then you have to decide on your destination. Should (3) <u>it</u> be in your country, near your country or do you want to travel to the other side of the world? Then perhaps you should think about what type of holiday you want. This decision is very important, and (4) <u>it</u> is often the one with the most different suggestions to consider – active holiday, beach holiday, city holiday, camping holiday, and so on. You also need to know how you want to travel. If you want to go a long way, then flying is probably your only option. But if you don't want to travel very far you have more options – car, bus or coach, train or you could even go on a bike! Last of all you should decide on a budget – how much do you want to spend? It's no good planning to fly to Australia in business class with some friends if you can't really afford to do that.

So, once you have sorted all these things out you can go to the travel agent's and get some information. Looking at travel brochures is the easiest thing in the world to do but they can also sometimes give you an overdose of information. It's better to talk to a travel agent first – and tell him or her what you really want. Then you can take the relevant information home with you, and take your time reading (5) <u>it</u> and thinking or talking about it.

It is hard for some of us to imagine, but some people don't like going on holiday. If you are one of those people, all you need to decide is how to spend your wonderful, relaxing two weeks at home. That decision could be much easier to make!

1 What is the text about?
a) ☐ holiday destinations   b) ☐ being on holiday   c) ☐ planning holidays

2 How many major decisions about going away on holiday does the text describe?
a) ☐ four   b) ☐ five   c) ☐ six

3 When should these decisions be made?
a) ☐ before seeing a travel agent   b) ☐ at the travel agent's   c) ☐ after seeing a travel agent

4 According to the text, how much information can travel brochures sometimes give you?
a) ☐ none   b) ☐ the right amount   c) ☐ too much

5 What should people who don't like going on holiday do?
a) ☐ force themselves to go   b) ☐ stay at home   c) ☐ see a doctor about it

2 Read the text again and decide what the five underlined words refer to.

1 ....   4 ....

2 ....   5 ....

3 ....

☐ out of **10**

Listening

1 🔊 L 48 You're going to hear part pf a conversation between a Diana and her husband, Paul.
Listen and decide if sentences 1 and 2 are true (✔) or not true (✘). Paul and Diana …

1 ☐ have booked their holiday.   2 ☐ agree to spend their holiday in America.

2 🔊 L 49 Listen again and decide if the statements 1–8 are true (✔) or not true (✘).

1 ☐ They have to decide about their summer holiday.
2 ☐ Paul lives in his home country.
3 ☐ Diana wants to stay in England this summer.
4 ☐ Paul doesn't really want to go to America again.
5 ☐ Diana wants to go to America for her sister's birthday.
6 ☐ Diana suggests going to Florida as part of the holiday.
7 ☐ Both Paul and Diana have been to Florida before.
8 ☐ Paul offers to get some brochures from the travel agent's.

☐ out of **10**

Language elements

1 Read this newspaper article. Decide which word or phrase is missing. Write a), b), or c), in the gaps.

Last month there (1) …. some visitors from China in our town. They (2) …. here (3) …. ten days. They (4)
…. welcomed by the town and especially by the people (5) …. they stayed with. They saw (6) …. new
things here, and they learnt (7) ….. about our way of life which, of course, (8) …. very different for them.
They had some English lessons here, and went on a trip (9) …. London where they (10) …. some of the
famous sights. They liked London but they (11) …. be (12) …. not to get lost! They are now in Germany
where they (13) …. visit Berlin, Cologne and then Munich. They (14) …. speak English there because they
(15) …. a word of German.

1 a) are, b) were, c) have been   10 a) have seen, b) were seeing, c) saw
2 a) have stayed, b) were staying, c) stayed   11 a) could, b) had to, c) have to
3 a) since, b) for, c) during   12 a) carefully, b) carelessly, c) careful
4 a) was, b) are, c) were   13 a) will, b) might, c) do a
5 a) who, b) whose, c) which   14 a) won't have to, b) won't be able to,
6 a) much, b) little, c) a lot of   c) will have to
7 a) something, b) anything, c) none   15 a) can't speak, b) aren't speaking,
8 a) are, b) is, c) will be   c) didn't speak
9 a) in, b) at, c) to

2 Write in the missing words.

1 The Chinese people came ……………………. our town for a visit.

2 Some English lessons ……………………. organised for them.

3 They (be) ……………….. …………………………. in Germany …………………. they left England.

4 English isn't ………………….. difficult to learn …………………. Chinese.

5 If they (know) …………………. a little German they'd

  (can) …………………. to practise it in Germany.

☐ out of **20**

🔑 p. 96

My result: ☐ out of **40**

Unit 1 **2** **Using English** page 10

🔊 **T 2** Listen to the conversation between Konrad and his new teacher.
Fill in the first words of the teacher's questions.

1 .... did you last have an English lesson?

2 .... was your last lesson?

3 .... did you learn English at school?

4 .... you ever speak English to anybody?

5 .... anybody in your family speak English?

6 .... you ever listen to English?

7 .... you having problems understanding me now?

8 .... do you want to come to an English class?

9 .... do you want to improve?

10 .... anybody else you know learning English at the moment?

🔊 **T 3** Listen again. Make a note of Konrad's answers. Just a few key words will do.

	Konrad's answers	My partner's answers
1		
2		
3		
4		
5		
6		
7		
8		
9		
10		

Act out the conversation with your partner. One of you should ask the teacher's questions and make a note of the other person's answers.

Change roles.

Unit 7 **2** Vocabulary check: Family members page 54

Who are the people in this family tree? For example, number 1 is Ted's father.

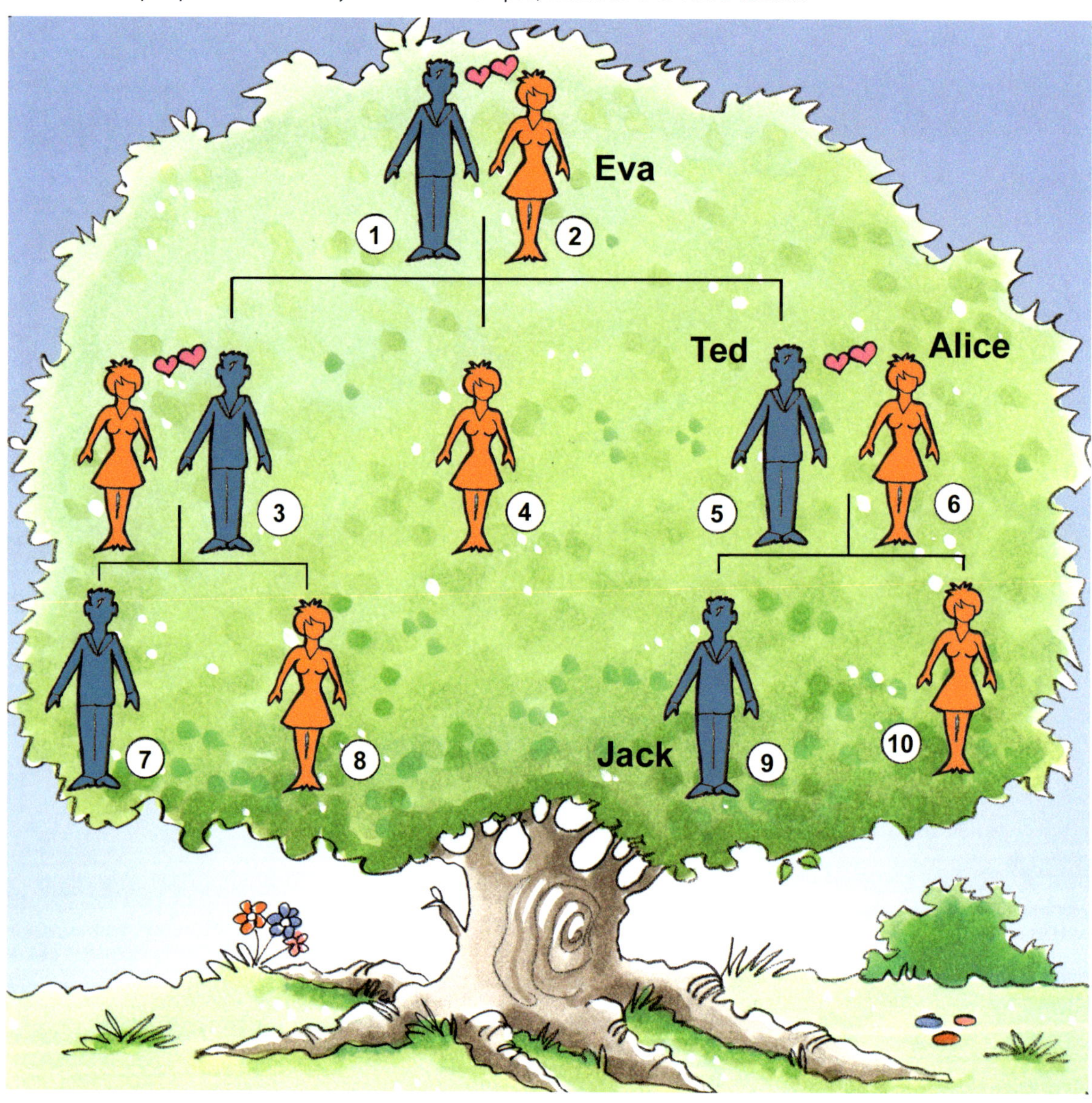

for Ted:	1	*father*
	2	
	3	
	4	
	7	
	8	
	10	
for Eva:	9	
	10	

for Alice:	1+2	
	3	
	4	
	9	
for Jack:	1+2	
	3	
	4	
	5+6	
	7+8	

You made a report on one of the break-ins that happened last weekend.

Tick: **three things that burglars broke**
four things that they stole *and*
three things that they ruined.

Partner A, write your ticks under A, and Partner B under B. **Important: Don't let your partner see your ticks!** Write numbers in the columns where possible, e.g. the number of windows that were broken.

	broke		stole		ruined	
	A	B	A	B	A	B
windows						
antique mirror						
bottles of rare whisky						
curtains						
carpets						
leather sofa						
antique statue						
original paintings						
crystal glasses						
DVD player						
TV						
laptop						
mobile phone						
iPod						
credit cards						
jewellery						
Rolex watch						
designer clothes						
large amount of cash						

Now find out what happened at the house that your partner went to. Ask questions like this: *Were any windows broken by the burglars? How many …? Was a … stolen?*
Record the information about your partner's burglary in the other column.

Now compare the two burglaries with your partner. Do you think they were done by the same person or people?

Unit 10 **Listen and discuss** page 73

These are the things that the students who have just finished their English course want to do in the future so that they can continue practising and learning. Tick the ones that you think you might be able to do, too.

The students who were in England:	You:
1 write e-mails to others in the class	
2 read the news on the internet (e.g. www.bbc.co.uk or www.cnn.com)	
3 read English newspapers and magazines	
4 work in an English-speaking country	
5 go travelling	
6 set up an informal conversation group	
7 do another course	
8 watch television	
9 buy a self-study course / self-study material	

Now talk to the others in your class about what you all think you might be able to do in the future. Have you got any other ideas? If you have, write them here:

Personal diary

The aim of the partner A/B file activities is to communicate with a partner and exchange information. So it's important that you don't look at your partner's page – you have to get the information you need by **talking** to each other.

Unit 2 **4** How to say it: Giving advice page 16

Take turns to describe a 'problem' and to give advice. These are your 'problems'. Choose some of them to tell your partner. He or she will give you some advice.

1 Your neighbours make a lot of noise late at night.
2 Your boss doesn't smell very nice.
3 Your children never put their things away in their rooms.
4 You haven't got any money and you need some quickly.
5 A colleague from work is coming to dinner and you don't know if he or she is vegetarian or not.
6 You bought a CD last week, but then found that you already had it at home. You've lost the receipt.
7 You're unhappy because you have to start work very early. Before, you could start when you wanted.
8 You want to sell your car, but you don't know how to do this.

Listen to your partner's 'problems'. Give him or her some advice. Use these expressions:
Why don't you …?   *I think you should … .*   *If I were you, I'd … .*

Unit 4 **5b** Comparing past James Bonds page 33

Ask your partner questions so that you can complete this information. You will need these words in your questions: *old, heavy, tall, colour.*

Name	Sean Connery	George Lazenby	Roger Moore	Timothy Dalton	Pierce Brosnan
Age	32–53	30	46–58		42–49
Eyes	brown		blue		blue
Hair	dark brown	brown		dark brown	
Weight	85kg		80kg		85kg
Height	1.89m	1.89m		1.85m	

Answer your partner's questions.

Now work together with your partner and write four sentences like this: *XX was / wasn't … .* Use all the actors' names at least once.

Your sentences should include the correct forms of these words:

1 *young* (comparative)
2 *old* (superlative)
3 *heavy* (superlative)
4 *not as tall* (comparative)

Unit 6 `6c` **Find someone who** page 45

- First, write the correct form of the verb in the gaps:

Find someone who has (ride) *ridden* .... a horse.

Find someone who has (eat) .... caviar.

Find someone who has (write) .... a letter in English.

Find someone who has (work) .... in an office.

Sandra

- Now ask questions beginning with *Have you ever …?* so that you can find these people in your class (if possible). Write their names in the boxes above. Try to have a different name in every box.

- When you have finished, go back to one of the people whose name you wrote down. Have a short conversation with him/her, like this. Make a note of the answers you get.

A: Sandra, you **have ridden** a horse, **haven't** you?

Sandra: Yes, I have.

A: Where **did** you last **ride** a horse?

Sandra: I rode a horse in the south of Spain.

A: And when **did** you last **ride** a horse?

Sandra: It was in May last year.

A: What colour **was** that horse?

Sandra: I think it was …

The aim of the partner A/B file activities is to communicate with a partner and exchange information. So it's important that you don't look at your partner's page – you have to get the information you need by **talking** to each other.

Unit 2   **4**   How to say it: Giving advice page 16

Take turns to describe a 'problem' and to give advice.

Listen to your partner's 'problems'. Give him or her some advice. Use these expressions:
Why don't you ...?   I think you should ... .   If I were you, I'd ... .

These are your 'problems'. Choose some of them to tell your partner. He or she will give you some advice

1 All the plants you buy die within two or three days.
2 The man in the next flat to you always smokes in the lift. It stinks.
3 You very often get headaches in the evenings.
4 You always feel hungry in the evening – just before you go to bed.
5 You'd like to find an old school friend who you haven't heard from for years.
6 You want to buy a television that is on special offer today only – but you haven't got a car.
7 You want to find a new flat, but you don't know the best way to do this.
8 You would like to have guest for dinner more often, but you don't feel very confident about cooking.

Unit 4   **5b**   Comparing past James Bonds page 33

Answer your partner questions about the James Bond actors.
Ask your partner questions so that you can complete the information below. You will need these words in your questions: *old, heavy, tall, colour.*

Name	Sean Connery	George Lazenby	Roger Moore	Timothy Dalton	Pierce Brosnan
Age	32–53	30		43–45	
Eyes	brown	brown		green	
Hair	dark brown		light brown		black
Weight	85kg	84kg		82kg	
Height	1.89m	1.89m	1.85m		1.84m

Now work together with your partner and write six sentences like this: *XX was / wasn't ... .* Use all the actors' names at least once.

Your sentences should include the correct forms of these words:

1 *young* (comparative)
2 *old* (superlative)
3 *heavy* (superlative)
4 *not as tall* (comparative)

Unit 6 `6c` **Find someone who** page 45

- First, write the correct form of the verb in the gaps:

  Find someone who has (ride) *ridden* .... a horse.

  Find someone who has (drink) .... champagne.

  Find someone who has (see) .... a live football match.

  Find someone who has (live) .... another country.

Paul

- Now ask questions beginning with *Have you ever …?* so that you can find these people in your class (if possible). Write their names in the boxes above. Try to have a different name in every box.

- When you have finished, go back to one of the people whose name you wrote down. Have a short conversation with him/her, like this. Make a note of the answers you get.

B: Paul, you **have ridden** a horse, **haven't** you?

Paul: Yes, I have.

B: Where **did** you last **ride** a horse?

Paul: I rode a horse in the south of Spain.

B: And when **did** you last **ride** a horse?

Paul: It was in May last year.

B: What colour **was** that horse?

Paul: I think it was …

Then tell your class what you know about the person that you spoke to, like this:
Paul has ridden a horse. He last rode one when he was in Spain on holiday in May last year. The horse …

Unit 1

Preview (page 9)

The second sentence.

Language study (page 12)

a) works, doesn't work, b) Do, live, don't, live, c) gets
d) are, doing, are doing, e) are making

Over to you (page 13)

1 1 speak / ~~are speaking~~, 2 ~~does~~ / is doing, 3 doesn't
use / ~~isn't using~~, 4 ~~goes out~~ / is going out, 5 speak /
~~are speaking~~, 6 ~~brush up~~ / are brushing up
7 Do, 8 Yes, they do. 9 Is, 10 No, he isn't. 11 Does,
12 No, he doesn't. 13 Does, 14 Yes, he does. 15 Are,
16 No, we aren't.

2 1g), 2d), 3e), 4a), 5h), 6c), 7f), 8b)

3 1) ~~13~~ / 30, 2) ~~16~~ / 60, 3) 12 / ~~20~~, 4) 18 / ~~80~~,
5) 89 / ~~98~~, 6) 108 / ~~180~~

4 1 smaller than, 2 of mixed ages, 3 years ago, 4 don't
use, 5 All

5 1c), 2d), 3b), 4e), 5a)
2, 5, 3, 1, 4

Vocabulary (page 103)

1 when, 2 why, 3 what, 4 which, 5 who, 6 whose, 7 how
long

Unit 2

Preview (page 15)

The third sentence is true.

Language study (page 18)

1b), 2a), 3c)
d) have … been living, have been living, e) has … been
working, has been working

Over to you (page 19)

1 1 does, 2 has (he) been taking, 3 have (the magazines)
been buying, 4 do
5 for, 6 for, 7 since, 8 for, 9 since, 10 for, 11 for,
12 since

2 1 photographer, photograph, 2 electrician, electricity,
3 adviser, advice, 4 politician, politics, 5 policeman,
police, 6 musician, music

3 1 apprentice, 2 full-time, 3 retired, 4 employer,
5 unemployed, 6 self-employed

4 1 a cook, 2 a circus clown, 3 a mountain guide,
4 a taxi driver

5 1 If I were you, I'd buy that one. 2 Why don't you buy
that one? 3 I think you should buy that one. 4 It might
be better to buy that one.
The reactions: 4, 1, 3, 2

Vocabulary (page 104)

1 a) to, b) in, c) of
2 a) at, b) for, c) after
3 a) in, b) on, c) at (AmE can be on the weekends)

Unit 3

Preview (page 21)

The first and second sentences are false. The third
sentence is true.

Language study (page 24)

1b), 2a), 3b), 4a), 5b), 6a)
If I suddenly became very rich, I would buy …

Over to you (page 25)

1 1 ~~she would have~~ / she had, she'd be able to go / ~~she
went~~, 2 ~~will you ask~~ / would you ask, you had to / ~~you
would want~~, 3 I didn't live / ~~I don't live, I can't~~ / I
wouldn't be able to, 4 if he had / ~~he has, he will never
have~~ / he would never have, 5 were, wouldn't work,
6 would be able to live, got, 7 wouldn't go, didn't
enjoy

2 1 I love …, 2 I enjoy …, 3 I quite like …, 4 I don't mind
…, 5 I don't really like …, 6 I'm not very keen on …,
7 I can't stand …, 8 I hate …,

3 2a) enjoy, 7b) can't stand, 5c) don't really like,
8d) hate, 6e) not very keen on, 1f) love, 7g) hate,
4h) don't mind

4 1 kitchen, 2 bedroom, 3 bathroom, 4 cellar, 5 living
room

5 1 <u>machine</u>, 2 weigh, 3 <u>cough</u>, 4 un<u>pleas</u>ant, 5 <u>cellar</u>

Vocabulary (page 105)

1 to, 2 on, 3 out, 4 up, 5 on, 6 out, 7 at, 8 up

Extra A

Vocabulary (page 30): 1 advertisement (advert, ad),
2 full-time, 3 mother tongue, 4 unimportant, 5 trial,
6 contract, 7 experience, 8 accommodation, 9 negotiable,
10 applicant

Unit 4

Preview (page 31)

The first and the third sentences are false, the second
and the fourth sentences are true.

Language study (page 34)

Noun: actor, adjective: good
Verb: act, adverb: well
His car was cheaper than mine.
John's boss works harder than John.

Over to you (page 35)

1 1 He's a <u>great</u> actor. He speaks (clearly) and he always gets on (well) with all the actors. He's a <u>good</u> singer, too.
2 James Bond always drives (fast) and sometimes rather (dangerously) in his films. Of course, he always gets <u>fast</u> cars to drive, and – after all – who would want to see a 'careful' James Bond?
3 than, more, 4 as, the most, 5 bad, badly, worse, the worst

2 1 age, 2 weight, 3 height, 4 centre, 5 hall, 6 school, 7 house

3 1 at<u>tract</u>ive, 2 <u>popul</u>ar, 3 <u>aggress</u>ive, 4 <u>danger</u>ous, 5 un<u>happy</u>, 6 con<u>vinc</u>ing

4 1 nightclub, 2 opera house, 3 stadium, 4 restaurant, 5 fitness centre, 6 theatre

5 1a) Yes, I would. Thank you very much. b) I'd love to, but I'm afraid I can't. 2 a) Oh, that's nice. Thanks, I'd love to come. b) I'm sorry, that's a pity. I'll be away at the weekend.

Vocabulary (page 106)

1 give a reason, 2 give an answer, 4 give a description, 6 give a dinner party

Unit 5

Preview (page 37)

How much money …, How many hours …, How many angels …, How much free wall space …

Language study (page 40)

things, places, people

Over to you (page 41)

1 Uncountable nouns: advice, bread, furniture, help, information, money, news, time
1 many / ~~much~~, ~~little~~ / a few / ~~none~~, 2 ~~a~~ / any / some, anything / ~~something~~, 3 a / ~~any~~ / ~~some~~, ~~a little~~ / any / a few, 4 ~~an~~ / ~~many~~ / some, ~~many~~ / much, 5 a / ~~some~~ / any, ~~a few~~ / a little, 6 ~~somewhere~~ / anywhere, ~~anywhere~~ / nowhere

2 1 our / hour, 2 there / their, 3 here / hear, 4 two / too

3 1 blue, 2 red, 3 yellow, 4 green, 5 white, 6 brown

4 1 a house, 2 a flat, 3 a shop with a flat above it, 4 a bungalow

6 1d), 2f), 3a), 4b), 5c), 6e)

Vocabulary (page 107)

1 black, 2 brown, 3 green, 4 purple, 5 pink, 6 red, 7 yellow, 8 blue, 9 beige, 10 white

Unit 6

Preview (page 43)

yes, no, yes, no

Language study (page 46)

a) were, was, b) did, go, went, didn't go, c) saw, haven't seen, d) went, has, been, e) sold, have, bought

Over to you (page 47)

1 1b), 2d), 3g), 4f), 5h), 6c), 7a), 8e)
9 went, 10 has never seen, 11 left, 12 didn't like, 13 has just started, 14 has already met, 15 hasn't been

2 Austrian, Australian, Brazilian, Italian, Canadian

3 1 They used to play <u>tennis</u> – but they've never played squash. 2 They used to <u>play</u> tennis – but now they watch it on TV. 3 <u>They</u> used to play tennis – but their son didn't. 4 They <u>didn't use</u> to play tennis – but they do now. 5 They <u>used</u> to play tennis – but they don't anymore.

4 1 Shall we stay at home? 2 Let's stay at home. 3 Why don't we stay at home?
6a) didn't agree to go, 3b) agreed to go, 5c) didn't agree to go, 7d) agreed to go, 4e) agreed to go, 1f) didn't agree to go, 2g) agreed to go

5 1 sports reporter, 2 manager, 3 sponsor, 4 trainer, 5 referee

Vocabulary (page 108)

1 never, 2 ever, 3 already, 4 not … yet, 5 just

Extra B

Your hotel room (page 52):
type of room: non-smoking room, executive suite
where the room is: on the ground floor, on the first floor, on the top floor
in your room: Internet access, mini-bar, TV
the bathroom: with a shower, with a bath
the bed: double bed, single bed, twin beds

Unit 7

Preview (page 53)

was having, left, was sitting, said

Language study (page 56)

3a), 4b), 1c), 2d)
was listening, were … doing, was watching

Over to you (page 57)

1 1 were waiting / ~~waited~~, ~~was coming~~ / came, ~~were saying~~ / said, 2 ~~was seeing~~ / saw, was walking / ~~walked~~, ~~was calling~~ / called, ~~was stopping~~ / stopped, 3 was doing / ~~did do~~, was listening / ~~listened~~, ~~was she doing~~ / did she do, ~~was answering~~ / answered 4 true, 5 true, 6 false, 7 true, 8 false, 9 false, 10 true, 11 true, 12 true

2 1 How did you feel about that? 1d), 2a), 3b), 4c)

3

sister, sister-in-law	brother, brother-in-law
mother, grandmother, aunt	father, grandfather, uncle
daughter, granddaughter, niece	son, grandson, nephew

4

d	t	id
opened	asked	expected
poured	laughed	wanted
ordered	grabbed	

5 1 relieved, 2 shocked, 3 annoyed, 4 sad, 5 delighted

Vocabulary (page 109)

sister, brother, son, daughter, husband, wife, father, mother, parents, children, nephew, niece, aunt, uncle, grandparents, grandmother, grandfather, sister-in-law, …
1 by, 2 about, 3 about, 4 by, 5 about, 6 about, 7 by/about, 8 about, 9 by/about, 10 by, 11 in, 12 of

Unit 8

Preview (page 59)

is, were, was, are

Language study (page 62)

Present passive: is, are
Past passive: was, were

Over to you (page 63)

1 1 was written, 2 are cleaned, 3 was drunk, 4 Were … printed, 5 was sung, 6 were designed, 7 was discovered, 8 are spent

2 1 at a station, 2 at a breakfast table, 3 in a coin dealer's shop, 4 in a bank, 5 in a restaurant a) 5, b) 1, c) 2

3 1 ~~mustn't~~ / don't have to, 2 ~~Chinese~~ / speak Chinese, 3 mustn't / ~~don't have to~~, 4 swim / ~~to swim~~

4 1 <u>qu</u>antity, 2 <u>unnecess</u>ary, 3 <u>cert</u>ai<u>n</u>ly, 4 <u>pro</u>ject, 5 k<u>now</u>

5 1 earn, 2 inherit, 3 invest, 4 lend, 5 save, 6 spend, 7 waste

Vocabulary (page 110)

1 head, 2 ear, 3 neck, 4 shoulder, 5 back, 6 hand, 7 finger, 8 thumb, 9 foot, 10 ankle, 11 leg, 12 elbow, 13 knee, 14 toe, 15 arm, 16 chest, 17 chin, 18 mouth, 19 nose, 20 eye

Unit 9

Preview (page 65)

1 Sunday afternoon, 2 Monday at 6 p.m., 3 ~~she'll see~~ / she won't see, 4 she'll be / ~~she won't be~~

Language study (page 68)

Future simple (will): 1c), 2a), 3b)
First conditional: won't be / is, don't come / will miss

Over to you (page 69)

1 1 will, will (be) able, 2 am, will (certainly) take, 3 won't, don't, 4 might, won't, 5 not, have

2

a **k** sound	an **s** sound	a **sh** sound
historical	since	special
costumes	celebration	
country	century	

3 Down under: 1, 3, 4, 6, 7. In Europe: 2, 5, 8

4 1 January, 2 Tuesday, 3 Wednesday, 4 Thursday, 5 Friday, 6 Saturday, 7 July

5 1 100%, 2 50%, 3 90%, 4 100%, 5 50%, 6 90%

Vocabulary (page 111)

1 Neujahr, 2 Karfreitag, 3 Ostersonntag, 4 Ostermontag, 5 Heiligabend, 6 erster Weihnachtsfeiertag, 7 zweiter Weihnachtsfeiertag, 8 Silvester, 9 Jahrestag, Jubiläum, 10 Geburtstag, 11 Hochzeit, 12 Hochzeitstag

Unit 10

Preview (page 71)

1 future, 2 present, 3 present, 4 future, 5 present, 6 future

Over to you (page 75)

1 1 are … going, 2 will … be, 3 does … leave, 4 Will … send, find, 5 will meet, 6 Are … going … stay, 7 might phone

2 1b), 2a), 3e), 4d), 5c)

3 1 newspaper, magazine, poster, Internet, 2 radio, friend, neighbour, 3 television

4 3 no, 4 yes, 5 no, 6 yes, 7 yes, 8 no, 9 yes

5 1 hope, 2 love, 3 want, 4 dream

Vocabulary (page 112)

1 colleagues, 2 friends, 3 neighbours, 4 newspapers,
5 notice boards, 6 magazines, 7 posters, 8 radio,
9 television

1   a) into, b) on, c) of, d) in
2   a) at, b) by, c) from, d) in

Extra C (page 80)

cardinal numbers: eight, fourteen, thirty-one, a/one
hundred and six, one thousand three hundred and
seventy
ordinal numbers: first, second, third, fourth, fifth, twelfth
dates: the twenty-second of February, the eighteenth of
March
years: nineteen ninety-nine, two thousand and six
telephone numbers: four oh nine six eight three, three
double six seven two oh
fractions: a half, a quarter, a third, two hundredths
decimals: two point three, five point one
percentages: twenty percent
temperatures: five degrees Celsius, minus two degrees
Celsius, sixty degrees Fahrenheit

Test yourself 1 (pages 81–82)

Reading

1   1c), 2b), 3f), 4i), 5h)
2   1c), 2b), 3a), 4c), 5c)

Listening

1   1 ✔, 2 ✗, 3 ✗, 4 ✗, 5 ✔
2   1 ✗, 2 ✔, 3 ✔, 4 ✗, 5 ✗

Language elements

1   line 1: o), d), h), line 2: b), n), a), line 3: k), c), f),
     line 4: j), line 5: i), l), line 6: g), e), line 7: m)
2   1) What's her job? 2) How long has she been working
     there? 3) Where is the hotel? 4) Why does she like her
     boss? 5) Where does she live?

Test yourself 2 (pages 83–84)

Reading

1   1 c), 2 b), 3 a), 4 c), 5 b)
2   1 planning a holiday, 2 the holiday, 3 the holiday
     destination, 4 the decision about the type of holiday,
     5 the relevant information

Listening

1   1 ✗, 2 ✔
2   1 ✔, 2 ✔, 3 ✗, 4 ✔, 5 ✗, 6 ✔, 7 ✗, 8 ✗

Language elements

1   1 b), 2 c), 3 b), 4 c), 5 a), 6 c), 7 a), 8 b), 9 c), 10 c),
     11 b), 12 c), 13 a), 14 c), 15 a)
2   1 to, 2 were, 3 have been, since, 4 as, as, 5 knew, be
     able

Information for the teacher

Unit 5, Exercise 4a (page 39)

Countable and uncountable nouns: *advice, book, bread, child, dollar, English, furniture, hour, idea, information,
money, news, newspaper, problem, time, woman*

Unit 6, Exercise 6a (page 45)

Irregular verbs: *buy, drink, drive, eat, make, meet, ride, see, speak, write*

Extra B, Task 1 (page 49)

1 Which American president was shot in Texas?
2 Which American president was born in Texas?
3 Which famous gangster was a Texan?
4 Which animal farmers are typical of Texas?
5 Which is the biggest state in the USA?
6 What is the state capital of Texas?
7 Which of these neighbours of Texas is a country?
8 Which famous building is in Texas?
9 Where are the beaches of Texas?
10 What is the state dish of Texas?
11 What is the most popular sport in Texas?
12 What is the most famous product from under the ground in Texas?

Unit 1, Exercise 3: Pronunciation (page 13)

1 She's got 30 kids in her class.
2 I think she lives at number 60.
3 He started working there about 12 years ago.
4 He'll be 18 next year.
5 My grandmother was 89 when she died.
6 There are 108 different things on the menu at the Chinese restaurant.

Unit 1, Exercise 4: Listening (page 13)

(KT = Konrad's teacher / OT = other teacher)

OT: Well, that's the first lesson over and done with. How was your class? You've got that new course, haven't you?
KT: Yeah, the Refresher course. They were fine, we had a really nice lesson. I've got the feeling they'll be a very good group.
OT: Mm, mine too. How many have you got?
KT: Erm, there were eleven here tonight. That's a good number. Last time I found that eighteen was … well … too many. The room is too small for so many anyway.
OT: My class is quite small, too – only eight at the moment. But eight teenagers is probably enough!
KT: Yeah, I think I'd rather have eight senior citizens than eight teenagers – not that I've got anything against teenagers, of course. My lot are all ages now – from about mid-twenties to … erm … well, I don't know really – but there are a couple of senior citizens, too.
OT: That's a nice mixture to have.
KT: Yes. They've all had some English before but a long time ago. They're all a bit rusty at the moment.
OT: Mm, I suppose everybody needs English for their jobs nowadays.
KT: Yes, that's probably true. But in *this* group, most of them need it for travel and families and so on. Only one or two need it for work.
OT: Well, I expect you'll make them all work hard, you usually do!
KT: Oh, yes – but they want to work hard. We talked about the course and they all agreed together – that if they all work at it – and that includes doing the homework – then the class will get a lot out of the course. So, they're a great team already.
OT: Certainly sounds like it. Oh, time for the next class. What have you got now?
KT: Oh, I've finished for today. I'm off home now.
OT: OK, see you next week then.
KT: Yeah, bye.

Unit 2, Exercise 3: Vocabulary (page 19)

1 a young person who is learning a job and working at the same time is an …
2 a job where you work about 40 hours a week is a … job

3 a … person is someone used to work, but is over 60 and doesn't work now
4 the person who you work for is your …
5 someone who could work, but hasn't got a job is …
6 someone who works for himself or herself is …

Unit 2, Exercise 4: Listening (page 19)

1 *(M = man, W = woman)*
M: … and what do you think are the other important things in this job?
W: I think presentation is really important. It must look good and smell good – that is so important.
M: Yes, you're right there. Good presentation is really important.

2 *(W = woman, M = man)*
W: … and do you like children? That is, of course, absolutely necessary …
M: Like children – I love 'em. I've got three of my own.
W: And you don't mind if people laugh at you all the time.
M: No, of course not – that's part of the job, isn't it?

3 *(W = woman, M = man)*
W: … and have you done some training in first aid? Would you be able to help a person who fell or who suddenly felt ill?
M: Oh yes, I have done several courses in first aid. I know how important it is.
W: Tell, me – why is it so important?
M: Well, I could be miles away from anywhere and then I'd the *only* person who could help. It would be an absolute disaster if I didn't know what to do.

4 *(M = man, W = woman)*
M: … so now why exactly do you want to do this job?
W: Well, I want to be able to help people. Everybody needs some help at some time.
M: How do you think you would be *helping* people in this job?
W: Well, we all know what it's like to arrive in a strange place, and not know the language or where anything is. It can be quite stressful. I would try to make visitors feel relaxed and at home as soon as they arrive here.

Unit 3, Exercise 3: Listening (page 25)

(Co = Colin, Cl = Claire)
Co: Oh, hi Claire. Erm … come on in.
Cl: I'm not interrupting anything, am I? I thought I heard …
Co: Oh yes, yes – that was just me being domesticated. I mean … now … that I'm living alone things are a bit different. But I'm afraid I'm not very good at all these domestic things. Cup of tea? I'm good at that.

Cl: Yeah – thanks.

Co: I mean, I like cooking. Well, I enjoy 'creating' in the kitchen! if you know what I mean. I can cook two or three different things now. But I *hate* shopping for food. All those people and babies and things – it's just too awful. I can't stand walking around supermarkets.

Cl: With me it's exactly the opposite. I *really* like going to food shops and I *love* buying special things. Trouble is – I always spend too much money! But I don't really like cooking – I'm just no good at it. And then there are the things you have to do *after dinner* or the next day or sometime. They just ruin the whole thing.

Co: Like what?

Cl: Well, for one thing, I really dislike emptying the dishwasher. Don't ask me why. I know the things are nice and clean and it only takes five minutes – dadada – but I hate it. But even worse is taking the rubbish out. It's always a bit stinky and …

Co: No, I'm not very keen on taking the rubbish out, either. I can never remember which day it is that they come to get it. But – ah – the dishwasher – that's quite different.

Cl: Don't tell me you like emptying the dishwasher!

Co: No … that's just it … I … I … haven't got one.

Cl: Oh, I see. Look, isn't there anything more interesting for us to talk about than *housework*?

Co: No, no … don't forget this is all new to me – I'm ashamed to say that my ex used to do all those awful things like shopping and ironing …

Cl: Ironing! I *love* ironing. I always watch television while I'm doing it, or listen to music … that's nice. It's quite relaxing. And you?

Co: Erm … I don't do it. Now I always wear shirts that don't need ironing, and well … I don't iron my bedclothes, so … no, definitely not a topic for me.

Cl: Okay … what about gardening then?

Co: Working in the garden? Oh, Claire – you know I haven't got a garden anymore.

Cl: Oh yes, right – sorry. Well, with me you can't call it gardening … on my small balcony, and anyway … there's nothing at all on my balcony.

Co: What happened to that tomato plant I gave you?

Cl: Sorry, it died. I never remembered to water it.

Co: Oh, don't worry – all my plants die, too. They don't get enough light in here …

Cl: Well, you could try cleaning the windows, perhaps.

Co: Now that's one thing I *really* hate doing.

Cl: Oh, do you? I quite like cleaning my windows … I only do it twice a year, but I do enjoy it. It's great when you can actually see through them again. But I hate cleaning the bathroom … oh, and the car, too. Awful! It always takes me such a long time to do it.

Co: Okay – you can come and clean my windows because I hate doing that … and I'll clean your car –

I don't mind cleaning cars, in fact I quite enjoy it. What do you think?

Cl: I think we need another cup of tea.

Co: Okay, coming up.

Cl: But you've started me thinking now. Good idea to get someone else to do the things you don't like doing. Colin … do you happen to like …

Unit 4, Exercise 4: Listening (page 35)

1 It was great but it was very, very loud. The disc jockey was Spanish and he was really good. They also had fantastic lights there. I enjoyed it, but I've got a bit of a headache. We danced for hours.

2 I think it was probably the best performance of La Traviata that I've ever seen. The soprano was absolutely superb.

3 Well, I've never been to a match – 22 men running around after one ball – that doesn't really interest me at all. But yesterday I went with my nephew, and it was a real surprise to me. It was a great match and I enjoyed the atmosphere there. Nobody won though – in the end it was a draw: 2–2.

4 It was lovely – very romantic. We had a table in the corner and there were flowers and a candle on the table. Just lovely.

5 I didn't think I'd enjoy it very much – you know … all those fantastic bodies in lycra. But yesterday evening was a sort of open evening for people who'd never been there before. They showed us the place and showed us some of the equipment and the exercises you can do on them. Some of them look a bit too much like hard work, but … these extra kilos just have to go.

6 I only went because Sophie had a spare ticket. I'm not really into all that classical stuff – those plays are sometimes just too long. But the actors were so good, they really were. I don't know how they do it – you know, the same story night after night. I don't think I could do that – but I wouldn't be able to remember the lines, anyway.

Unit 5, Exercise 4: Listening (page 41)

1 *(EA = estate agent, M = man)*

EA: Yes, I thought I'd better phone you immediately. I've got a wonderful new property. We only received the details last week.

M: I hope it's nice and quiet. It is detached, isn't it?

EA: Yes, it's detached so you won't be able to hear any noise from the neighbours – they're not very close to your property, I mean this property.

M: Yes, and what about the size of the rooms?

EA: They're a good size – there are two very big living rooms downstairs – and upstairs you've got four bedrooms, although two of them are quite small.

M: Oh dear, I'm not sure that that will be enough for us
    ...
EA: Well if you need another bedroom – you could build
    an extra room over the garage – that wouldn't be a
    problem at all.
M: Yes, that's an idea, I suppose. And what about the
    garden?
EA: Hm, the garden's not in very good condition, I'm
    afraid – you'd have to get some professionals in to
    see to that, I think. Do you think you'd like to ...

2 *(EA = estate agent, W = woman)*

EA: It's a really nice place. The rooms are big and so is
    the kitchen and bathroom – even the entrance is a
    fair size.
W: What about the other people in the building? Would
    I have families and children next door to me?
EA: There aren't any neighbours next to you – each
    property occupies one whole floor. And there are no
    neighbours to disturb you from above either, as this
    place is at the top.
W: Oh, at the top of the building, that sounds good.
EA: The only problem as far as I can see is that there is
    no outside space at all – no garden and no balcony.
    But the views are great. Would it matter an awful lot
    that there isn't ...

3 *(EA = estate agent, W = woman)*

W: I thought I'd just give you a ring again ...
EA: I'm glad you've called. I've got a new property here
    that I think is absolutely ideal for you. The best thing
    about it is the position.
W: Where is it?
EA: It's in George Street, and that would be perfect for
    your business. Hundreds of people walk through
    George Street on their way to the station and they'd
    see the things in your window every day. Couldn't be
    better, really.
W: Yes, I must say – that all sounds good. And the rest
    of the property?
EA: The upstairs accommodation isn't very big – but it's
    only you and your husband, isn't it? And it isn't too
    expensive so perhaps you could also afford to rent a
    ...

4 *(EA = estate agent, M = man)*

EA: Yes, that's right. Now I also remember you telling me
    that your knees aren't too good, and so you can't
    walk up and down stairs very well. Well, this
    property, hasn't got any stairs – and you can go
    directly out into the garden which was something
    else you wanted, if I remember correctly.
M: That sounds good. Does the garden get the sun?
EA: Yes, the place is in a very nice position – you get the
    morning sun on the side where the bedroom is and
    in the afternoon you've got full sun into the living
    room and the garden.

M: Sounds like the perfect place for me. No stairs, lots
    of sun, nice garden.
EA: Would you like to go and see it?
M: Yes, when do you think we could make an
    appointment ...

Unit 6, Exercise 3: Pronunciation (page 47)

1 They used to play <u>tennis</u> – but they've never played
    squash.
2 They used to <u>play</u> tennis – but now they watch it on
    TV.
3 <u>They</u> used to play tennis – but their son didn't.
4 They <u>didn't use</u> to play tennis – but they do now.
5 They <u>used</u> to play tennis – but they don't anymore.

Unit 6, Exercise 4: How to say it (page 47)

1 The cinema? That would be great, but I'm sorry –
    I'm busy on Friday.
2 The cinema? Good idea. What time?
3 The cinema? Well, I'd rather go to the theatre, but hey
    no – I'll come to the cinema with you instead.
4 The cinema? Well, actually I had planned to stay at
    home. But an evening out sounds much better, I must
    say.
5 The cinema? Yes, I'd like too, but well, I'm not sure –
    let's leave it for a while, shall we?
6 The cinema? You know I'd love to see that film, but
    I've got to work late – I just haven't got the time.
7 The cinema? Well, as you know I usually prefer to
    watch films on DVD at home – but *King Kong* – well,
    I'd really like to see it in the cinema – the special
    effects are great.

Unit 6, Exercise 5: Listening (page 47)

1 The good part about the job is that you always get
    tickets to the big matches and you often get special
    treatment. At really big matches there are a lot of us
    there. I also enjoy the opportunity to be able to
    interview the top people – that's great.
2 I look after the business side of things. There are a lot
    things to organise for the team and for individual
    players, too. I have to make sure that their contracts
    are okay and that they do everything they should do.
    My team is quite small – with a big team, this is an
    enormous job.
3 My company wants to support the players, of course
    ... but if we're honest, the most important thing for us
    is the advertising potential. We're very happy when
    we see our name everywhere during the tournaments
    – this can be on the players' clothes – that's very
    good for TV, in the sports halls – or in the
    programmes that people buy. We're lucky that most
    players like our products.
4 During the matches, I sit on the side and watch how
    they're playing. I make notes on what they're doing
    and then I can sometimes give them some tips at

half-time. But most of my work goes on during the rest of the week – hard physical work for me and for them.

5 It isn't an easy job, you know. I very often have to make very fast decisions – and sometimes people don't like what I decide … not the players and not the crowd, either. That's hard.

Unit 7, Exercise 5: Listening (page 57)

1 I did my driving test yesterday morning. I didn't really feel very confident about it, at all – but I thought I'd give it try. And, that was just so good when he said I'd passed. I really didn't want to have to take more lessons.

2 I was out shopping yesterday when I saw this man with a small child. They were just coming out of a video shop. Suddenly the man started hitting this child and screaming at him. It was really awful. He hit him and hit him – I don't know if he was drunk. But I don't know why I didn't react. I was frozen to the spot – I just didn't move. I've never seen anything like it. My friend said my face was as white as anything.

3 So they phoned me up yesterday and said that they would come on Friday to have a look at it. So I asked what time they would come. They said that all they could say was Friday. I mean what do they think I am? I can't sit around all day just waiting for them to come. Why can't they give a time – or at least say morning or afternoon?

4 You know, I feel a bit silly really – but I loved that cat. He was with me for years. He was a real friend. I know he was ill and all that but I didn't want him to die. He wasn't really very old. I'll miss him terribly.

5 *(W = woman, M = man)*
W: It's absolutely fabulous, really great.
M: Yes, more than we ever hoped for.
W: I mean, when they said that we'd won a holiday – we thought it would be a weekend in Paris or something like that. And we would have been happy with that.
M: Yeah, sure – I mean a holiday is a holiday, isn't it?
W: But then when they phoned yesterday and said that it was the first prize – a safari holiday in Africa – I couldn't believe my ears.
M: Yes, great news – really great.
W: We're over the moon about it.

Unit 8, Exercise 2: Listening (page 63)

1 *(W = woman, M1 = first man, M2 = second man)*
W: Excuse me, have you got …
M1: Very sorry, can't stop. Please ask someone else.
W: Excuse me, can you help me? I've only got a £10 note … and I need …
M2: Ah .. for the machine … why don't they take notes? I don't know … it's always the same problem. What do you need exactly?

W: Some pounds and some smaller coins, I think … honestly, I don't know how tourists manage.
M2: No … here you are – a fiver and some coins, OK?
W: Thanks a lot – that's very kind of you.

2 *(M = mother, F = father)*
M: Well, why does he need more?
F: He says that all the others get more than him – and he doesn't think that's fair.
M: But why does he actually *need* more? That some people have more than others is, I'm afraid, a fact of life. And the sooner he learns that, the better.
F: Oh come on. Let's just make it a bit more. It doesn't have to be very much.
M: Oh, you boys … you always stick together … okay, I give in, we'll give him …

3 *(M1 = shop assistant, M2 = customer)*
M1: Hmm – well, these aren't of any interest to me. There are a lot of them about.
M2: So they aren't worth anything then.
M1: No, I'm afraid not. But this one here – is very nice. Yes, it's in excellent condition.
M2: Oh, good. Would you be interested in buying this then?
M1: Yes, I would. Give me a moment, please – I'll just show it to my colleague and see what she says. Please take a seat – I won't be a minute.
M2: Thank you. While I'm waiting, I'll have a look at those over there they're really very nice …

4 *(W = woman, M = man)*
W: I'm very sorry, Mr O'Neill, but we just can't give you that much now.
M: Why not?
W: I'm afraid that the large payment you were expecting hasn't arrived in your account yet.
M: No?
W: No – and without that … there's nothing we can do.
M: Now just a moment, I've been a customer here for the past …
W: Mr O'Neill, would you like to come through here, then we can speak more privately about this.
M: I don't want to speak more privately – I want the money – now.
W: This way please, Mr O'Neill. I'll ask our manager if he …

5 *(WA = waiter, W = woman, M = man)*
WA: Here you are, sir.
W: Oh, excuse me – but that's for me.
WA: Oh, very sorry madam – here you are.
W: Thank you. I don't know why they always think the man is going to pay.
M: Well, I suppose the man usually does … in most cases.
W: Oh really – not any more. They should wake up to the 21st century.

M: Yes, I suppose you're right. They should just ask who
     wants it.
W: Yes, that would be much better …

Unit 9, Exercise 2: Pronunciation (page 69)

1   a **k** sound: historical, costumes, country
2   a **s** sound: since, celebration, century
3   a **sh** sound: special

Unit 9, Exercise 3: Listening (page 69)

1   Well, the last thing that people would want is a
    traditional Christmas dinner – you know, roast turkey
    and all that, followed by Christmas TV.
2   I just love it when you look outside and it's all white
    and crisp.
3   It's all beach games and sun cream.
4   Must be strange that it doesn't get dark early – what
    about lights and candles and things?
5   I think it's really nice that the Christmas holiday time
    is so different from most people's main holiday in the
    year. One in winter, one in summer.
6   Father Christmas still walks around in his big red coat
    and long white beard – a bit surprising really. He must
    be boiling hot all the time.
7   What? No snow? Never? Nowhere?
8   We usually go to the park after our Christmas dinner –
    and if the lake is frozen all the kids go ice skating. It
    looks pretty.

Unit 10, Exercise 2: Listening (page 75)

(M = man, W = woman)
1
M: We're taking grandma to London to see a show on
    Saturday. Everything is already booked – the theatre,
    the train tickets and a taxi to the station, too.

2
W: Our train leaves here at 11.45 and gets to London at
    12.55. The show starts at 2.30 – so we've got plenty
    of time.

3
M: Do we need to get to the theatre early to pick up the
    tickets?
W: No, it's okay. I finish work at four on Friday, so I'll go
    to the theatre and get them on my way home.

4
M: If grandma isn't too tired after the show, perhaps we'll
    invite her to an early dinner in London, too, She'd like
    that.

5
W: And we're all going to have a quiet day at home on
    Sunday.

Unit 10, Exercise 4: Pronunciation (page 75)

1   Well, that's something to look forward to, isn't it?
    (rising intonation)
2   Well, that's something to look forward to, isn't it?
    (falling intonation)
3   They're performing a play by Oscar Wilde this
    weekend, aren't they? *(falling intonation)*
4   It's called The Importance of Being Earnest, isn't it?
    (rising intonation)
5   The show starts at 7.30, doesn't it?
    (falling intonation)
6   The theatre is near the university, isn't it?
    (rising intonation)
7   You haven't booked tickets yet, have you?
    (rising intonation)
8   It'll be a lovely evening out, won't it?
    (falling intonation)
9   We'll be able to get tickets on the night, won't we?
    (rising intonation)

Test yourself 1: Listening (page 82)

1   When I get up in the mornings, I always have a quick
    breakfast and leave the house in time to get the 7.30
    to the city. I meet a friend at the station, on the
    platform, and we travel to work together – it's nice to
    have someone to talk to. But I'm always happy at the
    weekend when, for two days, I don't *have* to go
    anywhere!
2   We're six mothers and we see each other most days
    when we take our children to school. Three of us have
    got two children and the other three have all got one.
    After that we often go for a coffee and sometimes we
    go for a walk or to the local swimming pool. We have
    to pick up the children again at lunchtime.
3   I'm an actor, and I'm between jobs, as they say. So I
    decided do some writing. I've been working on some
    short stories since my last acting job in the theatre –
    that was about four months ago. I'd like to have
    another two months so that I can finish my stories.
    Then I hope to go back to my 'real' job – perhaps get
    some work for television.
4   The most difficult thing about my job is sleeping.
    During that hot weather last week, everybody said it
    was too hot to sleep. But imagine what it was like for
    me. I often have to sleep during the day – when I'm
    on nights at the hospital. I mean, our office staff
    never work nights – but we do. Anyway, it's better
    now – it isn't as hot as it was.
5   I wouldn't change my way of life for anything. I love
    being on the road, driving somewhere in Europe for a
    week or two at a time. I drive down to the south coast
    – that takes me about half an hour – it's not very far
    from home – and then I cross the channel to France
    and then go on to Germany or Italy. It's a great life.

Tapescript

Test yourself 2: Listening (page 84)

(D = Diana, P = Paul)

D: I think we should decide very soon what we want to do in the summer.

P: Why's that?

D: Well, I promised my parents that we would visit them in July.

P: Do we have to?

D: Paul, that's an awful thing to say. You know I miss them. It's OK for you, we live in *your* country – you can see your family whenever you want.

P: But do we have to go to America *again?* I'd like to do something different. We could stay here in England, or we could go south – to Spain, for example.

D: Yes, that would be lovely. But you know I want to go back home this summer. My sister's getting married and I want to be there.

P: But look, I got these brochures this morning at the travel agent's. This one's on Spain and Portugal and this one on southwest England – Devon and Cornwall.

D: Paul, I'd really like to go to southwest England, You know I've never seen that part of the country. In fact, there's a lot of England that I haven't seen. But this year I want to go to back to Washington. It isn't just because that's where I've spent most of my life …

P: … it's the wedding.

D: … yes.

P: Okay … but when the wedding's over, let's take a real holiday somewhere – I just don't want to spend all the time visiting people.

D: Good idea – we could go to Florida, it's one of my favourite holiday destinations. I've been there many times, but it'd be new for you.

P: Hmm – Florida.

D: You'll love it – I'm sure you will. *Please* say yes, Paul.

P: Okay – you win. Yes.

D: Great – I'll go to the travel agent's tomorrow and get some information … and then we can book.

P: And when *is* the wedding exactly?

D: At the end of July – well, no, actually we'd have to *travel* at the end of July – it's on the 3ʳᵈ August.

P: Hmm – yes, that's okay – I *can* take my holiday then. Right … let's do it!

D: Thank you – it means so much to me.

P: Oh? That much?

Phonetische Umschrift

englischer Laut		ähnlicher deutscher Laut
[ɪ]	in	*in*
[e]	yes	*fett*
[æ]	thanks	zwischen *a* und *ä*
[ʌ]	come	*machen*
[ɒ]	coffee	*Motte*
[ʊ]	look	*Butter*
[ə]	number	*singe*
[iː]	meet	*Knie*
[ɑː]	father	*Bahn*
[ɔː]	four	wie *o* in deutsch *Borke*
[uː]	too	*Buch*
[ɜː]	early	*Börse*
[eɪ]	day	nicht wie deutsch *ei* sondern [e] + [ɪ]
[aɪ]	nice	*Eile*
[ɔɪ]	boy	*heute*
[aʊ]	how	*Frau*
[əʊ]	no	[ə] + [ʊ]

englischer Laut		ähnlicher deutscher Laut
[ɪə]	here	*hier*
[eə]	where	*sehr*
[ʊə]	tourist	[ʊ] + [ə]
[v]	have	*Virus*
[θ]	thanks	wie ein gelispeltes *ss* in *Biss*
[ð]	this	wie ein gelispeltes *s* in *Sand*
[s]	seat	*Muße*
[z]	please	*Museum*
[ʃ]	she	*Schiff*
[ʒ]	television	*Regie*
[tʃ]	cheers	*klatschen*
[dʒ]	German	[d] + [ʒ]
[ŋ]	song	*singen*
[l]	old	hinten im Mund gesprochen
[j]	unit	*ja*
[w]	we	durch die Lippen gesprochen wie [uː]
[r]	repeat	vorn im Mund gesprochen

[ː] der vorangehende Laut wird lang gesprochen

[ˈ] Hauptbetonung: die folgende Silbe wird stark betont

[ˌ] Nebenbetonung: die folgende Silbe wird leicht betont

Unit 1 (pages 9–11)

Highlight the words you'd like to learn.

both [bəʊθ] beide
country ['kʌntrɪ] Land
different ['dɪfrənt] verschieden
difficult ['dɪfɪkəlt] schwierig
experience [ɪk'spɪərɪəns] Erfahrung
(a) few [(ə) 'fjuː] ein paar, einige
foreign language [ˌfɒrən'læŋgwɪdʒ] Fremdsprache
golf course ['gɒlf ˌkɔːs] Golfplatz
improve [ɪm'pruːv] verbessern
mean [miːn] meinen

opportunity [ˌɒpə'tjuːnətɪ] Gelegenheit, Chance
practise ['præktɪs] üben
probably ['prɒbəblɪ] vermutlich, wahrscheinlich
sell [sel] verkaufen
slowly ['sləʊlɪ] langsam
take photos [ˌteɪk 'fəʊtəʊz] Bilder machen
wear [weə] tragen (Kleidung)

Info (page 12)

destination [ˌdestɪ'neɪʃən] Ziel
government ['gʌvnmənt] Regierung

half [hɑːf] die Hälfte
level ['levəl] Niveau
particularly [pə'tɪkjʊləlɪ] besonders, vorzugsweise
(a) quarter [(ə) 'kwɔːtə] (ein) Viertel
retirement [rɪ'taɪəmənt] Ruhestand, Pensionierung
skills [skɪlz] Fähigkeiten, Fertigkeiten, Kenntnisse
survey [sə'veɪ] Studie
try [traɪ] versuchen

Word group: Verbs in instructions

circle ['sɜːkl] einkreisen
compare [kəm'peə] vergleichen
complete [kəm'pliːt] vervollständigen
decide [dɪ'saɪd] entscheiden
find out [faɪnd 'aʊt] herausfinden
listen ['lɪsən] zuhören
talk [tɔːk] reden, sprechen, unterhalten
tell [tel] erzählen
underline [ˌʌndə'laɪn] unterstreichen
write down [raɪt 'daʊn] aufschreiben, notieren

Word group: Fractions

half – (a) quarter

three quarters [ˌθriː 'kwɔːtəz] drei Viertel
a third [ə 'θɜːd] ein Drittel
two thirds [tʊ 'θɜːdz] zwei Drittel

Word group: Question words

Write in the question words:

1 wann ....

2 warum ....

3 was ....

4 welche ....

5 wer ....

6 wessen ....

7 wie lange ....

8 wie viel ....

9 wo ....

Word group: Countries and languages

England (English) – Spain (Spanish)

Austria (Austrian) ['ɒstrɪə ('ɒstrɪən)] Österreich
China (Chinese) ['tʃaɪnə (ˌtʃaɪ'niːz)] China
France (French) [frɑːns (frentʃ)] Frankreich
Germany (German) ['dʒɜːmənɪ ('dʒɜːmən)] Deutschland
Holland (Dutch) ['hɒlənd (dʌtʃ)] Holland
Italy (Italian) ['ɪtəlɪ (ɪ'tæljən)] Italien
Portugal (Portuguese) ['pɔːtʃʊgl (pɔːtʃu'giːz)] Portugal
Russia (Russian) ['rʌʃə ('rʌʃən)] Russland
Switzerland (Swiss) ['swɪtsələnd (swɪs)] Schweiz

✏ Writing task

You want to tell a friend about your English lesson. Write about what you did in Unit 1 beginning with:

First we talked about …

E-mail what you've written to someone in your class or give it to someone to read before the next lesson starts.

Words I need

....

....

....

....

⚷ p. 93

Unit 2 (pages 15–17)

Highlight the words you'd like to learn.

apprentice [ə'prentɪs] Auszubildende/r
area ['eərɪə] Gegend
boring ['bɔːrɪŋ] langweilig
challenge ['tʃælɪndʒ] Herausforderung
chase ['tʃeɪs] jagen
choir ['kwaɪə] Chor
close [kləʊs] nahe an
dangerous ['deɪndʒərəs] gefährlich
employed [ɪm'plɔɪd] angestellt
equipment [ɪ'kwɪpmənt] Ausrüstung
exciting [ɪk'saɪtɪŋ] aufregend
eye (of a hurricane) [aɪ] Zentrum (eines Hurrikans)
for [fɔː] seit
forecast ['fɔːkɑːst] Vorhersage

full-time [ˌfʊl 'taɪm] Vollzeit
hurricane ['herɪkʌn] Wirbelsturm
indoors [ɪn'dɔːz] im Haus
irregular [ɪ'regjʊlə] unregelmäßig
lightning ['laɪtnɪŋ] Blitz
opposite ['ɒpəzɪt] Gegenteil
past [pɑːst] vergangen, früher
part-time [ˌpɑːt 'taɪm] Teilzeit
present ['preznt] gegenwärtig
retired [rɪ'taɪəd] pensioniert
secure [sɪ'kjʊə] sicher
self-employed [ˌself ɪm'plɔɪd] selbständig
since [sɪns] seit
spend (time) [spend] verbringen
take photographs [ˌteɪk 'fəʊtəgrɑːfz] fotografieren
thunderstorm ['θʌndəstɔːm] Gewitter
towards [tə'wɔːdz] zu ... hin
train [treɪn] sich in Ausbildung befinden

unemployed [ˌʌnɪm'plɔɪd] arbeitslos
used to do ['juːst tə ˌduː] früher getan haben
(on its) way [ɒn ɪts weɪ] im Anzug

Info (page 18)

ad [æd] Inserat, Anzeige
advice [əd'vaɪs] Rat(schlag)
agency ['eɪdʒənsɪ] Agentur
claim [kleɪm] beantragen
government ['gʌvənmənt] Regierung
integrated ['ɪntɪgreɪtɪd] integriert
past [pɑːst] Vergangenheit
retraining [riː'treɪnɪŋ] Umschulung
service ['sɜːvɪs] Service
social security office ['səʊʃl sɪ'kjʊərətɪ 'ɒfɪs] Sozialamt
support [sə'pɔːt] Unterstützung
without [wɪð'aʊt] ohne

Word group: Adjectives describing jobs

boring – dangerous – exciting – stressful

demanding [dɪ'mɑːndɪŋ] anspruchsvoll
glamorous ['glæmərəs] glamourös
interesting ['ɪntrəstɪŋ] interessant
manual ['mænjʊəl] manuell
tiring ['taɪrɪŋ] anstrengend

Which words go where?

1 *in, of, to*

a) close .... the hurricane

b) interested .... weather

c) a photograph .... a storm

2 *after, at, for*

a) ansehen: look ....

b) suchen: look ....

c) sich kümmern um: look ....

3 *at, in, on*

a) .... the mornings

b) .... Mondays

c) .... the weekends

✎ Writing task

What do you think about Mike Theiss's job? Would you like to do his job?
Write about it beginning with:

I'd like to do Mike Theiss's job because ...
or
I wouldn't like to do Mike Theiss's job because ...

E-mail what you've written to someone in your class – or give it to someone to read before the next lesson starts.

Words I need

....
....
....
....
....
....
....
....

⟶ p. 93

Unit 3 (pages 21–23)

Highlight the words you'd like to learn.

appliance [əˈplaɪəns] Gerät, Vorrichtung
carpet [ˈkɑːpɪt] Teppich
cellar [ˈselə] Keller(geschoss)
chore [tʃɔː] (Routine)Arbeit, Pflicht
clean [kliːn] reinigen, sauber machen
companion [kəmˈpænjən] Gefährte / Gefährtin
cough [kɒf] husten
cupboard [ˈkʌbəd] Schrank
dirty [ˈdɜːtɪ] dreckig
disagree [ˌdɪsəˈgriː] widersprechen, anderer Meinung sein
empty [ˈemptɪ] (aus)leeren
enough [ɪˈnʌf] genug
feed [fiːd] füttern, ernähren
fridge [frɪdʒ] Kühlschrank
hangover [ˈhæŋəʊvə] Kater

introduce [ˌɪntrəˈdjuːs] vorstellen
iron [ˈaɪən] bügeln
key [kiː] Schlüssel
kitchen [ˈkɪtʃən] Küche
mess [mes] Unordnung
mirror [ˈmɪrə] Spiegel
prefer [prɪˈfɜː] vorziehen, lieber mögen
recharge [ˌriːˈtʃɑːdʒ] wieder aufladen
rubbish [ˈrʌbɪʃ] Abfall
shower [ˈʃaʊə] Dusche
smelly [ˈsmelɪ] muffig, übelriechend
spotty [ˈspɒtɪ] picklig
stray [streɪ] verirrt
take over [teɪk ˈəʊvə] übernehmen
untidy [ʌnˈtaɪdɪ] unordentlich
vacuum cleaner [ˈvækjuəm ˌkliːnə] Staubsauger
wardrobe [ˈwɔːdrəʊb] Kleiderschrank
weigh [weɪ] wiegen

Info (page 24)

building [ˈbɪldɪŋ] Gebäude
creator [krɪˈeɪtə] Erschaffer/in, Schöpfer/in
dangerous [ˈdeɪndʒərəs] gefährlich
examine [ɪgˈzæmɪn] untersuchen
explosives [ɪkˈspləʊsɪvz] Sprengstoff(e)
grass [grɑːs] Rasen
involvement [ɪnˈvɒlvmənt] Beteiligung, Verstrickung, Verwicklung
less [les] weniger
life [laɪf] Leben
manufacture [ˌmænjuˈfæktʃə] fertigen, produzieren
play [pleɪ] Theaterstück
real life [ˈrɪəl ˌlaɪf] wirkliches Leben
recent [ˈriːsənt] neuer, kürzlich
save [seɪv] retten

Word group: Rooms in a house

bathroom [ˈbɑːθruːm] Bad
bedroom [ˈbedruːm] Schlafzimmer
dining room [ˈdaɪnɪŋruːm] Esszimmer
kitchen [ˈkɪtʃən] Küche
living room [ˈlɪvɪŋruːm] Wohnzimmer
study [ˈstʌdɪ] Arbeitszimmer
toilet [ˈtɔɪlət] Toilette, WC

Which word goes where?

at, on, out, to, up

1 Introduce me ………… your friend.

2 It runs ………… batteries.

3 He always goes ………… on Fridays.

4 He woke ………… late yesterday.

5 I'm not very keen ………… ironing.

6 He never takes the rubbish ………… .

7 I don't like cooking ………… all.

8 Did he get ………… at 7 yesterday?

✏️ Writing task

Write a description of one of the rooms in your house or flat. Describe the things that are in it, too. Begin with:

My (room) is quite big. There are two large windows and …

or

My favourite room is …

E-mail what you've written to someone in your class – or give it to someone to read before the next lesson starts.

Words I need

....

....

....

....

....

....

....

....

⚷ p. 93

Unit 4 (pages 31–33)

Highlight the words you'd like to learn.

accept [əkˈsept] annehmen, akzeptieren

actor [ˈæktə] Schauspieler

angrily [ˈæŋgrəlɪ] wütend, verärgert

at least [ət ˈliːst] wenigstens

biographical [ˌbaɪəˈgræfɪkəl] biografisch

careful [ˈkeəfəl] vorsichtig

careless [ˈkeələs] unachtsam, nachlässig

cartoon [kɑːˈtuːn] Zeichentrickfilm

choose [tʃuːz] aussuchen, auswählen

convincingly [kənˈvɪnsɪŋlɪ] überzeugend

curly [ˈkɜːlɪ] lockig

dangerous [ˈdeɪndʒərəs] gefährlich

describe [dɪˈskraɪb] beschreiben

difference [ˈdɪfrəns] Unterschied

documentary [ˌdɒkjʊˈmentərɪ] Dokumentarfilm

enthusiastically [ɪnˌθjuːzɪˈæstɪklɪ] begeistert, enthusiastisch

heavy [ˈhevɪ] schwer

height [haɪt] Größe

(a) matter of opinion [(ə) ˈmætə əv əˈpɪnjən] (eine) Ansichtssache

neither … nor [ˈnaɪðə … nɔː] weder … noch

once [wʌns] einmal

politely [pəˈlaɪtlɪ] höflich

popular [ˈpɒpjələ] beliebt

population [ˌpɒpjʊˈleɪʃən] Bevölkerung

refuse [rɪˈfjuːz] sich weigern, ablehnen

regularly [ˈregjʊləlɪ] regelmäßig

sadly [ˈsædlɪ] traurig

similarity [ˌsɪməˈlærətɪ] Ähnlichkeit

slow [sləʊ] langsam

spend (free time) [spend] (Freizeit) verbringen

spy [spaɪ] Spion/in

star [stɑː] die Hauptrolle spielen

straight [streɪt] gerade

tall [tɔːl] groß

unlike [ʌnˈlaɪk] im Unterschied zu

war [wɔː] Krieg

weight [weɪt] Gewicht

wonder [ˈwʌndə] gern wissen wollen, sich fragen

young [jʌŋ] jung

Info (page 34)

concerned [kənˈsɜːnd] besorgt sein um

electricity [ɪˌlekˈtrɪsətɪ] Elektrizität

estimate [ˈestɪmeɪt] schätzen

government [ˈgʌvnmənt] Regierung

manufacturer [ˌmænjʊˈfæktʃərə] Hersteller

message [ˈmesɪdʒ] Botschaft, Nachricht

standby [ˈstændbaɪ] einsatzbereit, Standby

switch off [swɪtʃ ˈɒv] ausschalten

two thirds [tuːˈθɜːdz] zwei Drittel

Word group: Describing people

hair: curly – straight

long [lɒŋ] lang

short [ʃɔːt] kurz

wavy [ˈweɪvɪ] gewellt

dark (brown) [dɑːk (braʊn)] dunkel(braun)

light (brown) [laɪt (braʊn)] hell(braun)

body: tall – heavy

short [ʃɔːt] klein

light [laɪt] leicht

general: young – old

middle-aged [ˌmɪdlˈeɪdʒd] von mittlerem Alter

Where can the verb *give* go? Write it in four of these expressions.

1 .... a reason

2 .... an answer

3 .... a question

4 .... a description

5 .... an invitation

6 .... a dinner party

 p. 94

✏️ **Writing task**

Write a short paragraph about your all-time favourite film and the types of films that you like. Begin with:

I saw (name of film) years ago. It's my favourite because …

E-mail what you've written to someone in your class – or give it to someone to read before the next lesson starts.

Words I need

....

....

....

....

....

....

....

....

....

....

Unit 5 (pages 37–39)

Highlight the words you'd like to learn.

angel ['eɪndʒəl] Engel
appearance [ə'pɪrəns] Erscheinung
baroque [bə'rɒk] barock
candle ['kændl] Kerze
carpet ['kɑːpɪt] Teppich
castle ['kɑːsəl] Schloss
cherub ['tʃerəb] Cherub
curtain ['kɜːtən] Vorhang
decorate ['dekəreɪt] renovieren, dekorieren
difference ['dɪfrəns] Unterschied
furniture ['fɜːnɪtʃə] Möbel
grass [grɑːs] Gras, Rasen
home [həʊm] Heim
leisure facilities ['leʒə fə‚sɪlətɪs] Freizeitangebot
luckily ['lʌkɪlɪ] glücklicherweise
masterpiece ['mɑːstəpiːs] Meisterwerk

mirror ['mɪrə] Spiegel
need [niːd] Bedürfnis, Erfordernis
paint [peɪnt] Farbe
palace ['pæləs] Palast
piano [pɪ'ænəʊ] Klavier
pillar ['pɪlə] Säule, Pfeiler
prefer [prɪ'fɜː] vorziehen, lieber mögen
proudly ['praʊdlɪ] stolz
report [rɪ'pɔːt] berichten
(be) retired [(biː) rɪ'taɪəd] pensioniert, in Ruhestand sein
retirement [rɪ'taɪəmənt] Pensionierung, Ruhestand
roof [ruːf] Dach
sign [saɪn] Zeichen
space [speɪs] Raum, Platz
spend (money) [spend] (Geld) ausgeben
sports facilities [‚spɔːts fə'sɪlətɪs] Sportanlagen
transform [træns'fɔːm] umwandeln, transformieren

wall [wɔːl] Wand, Mauer
wish [wɪʃ] Wunsch

Info (page 40)

above [ə'bʌv] oberhalb
below [bɪ'ləʊ] below
deal with ['diːl wɪð] erledigen
estate agent [ɪ'steɪt ‚eɪdʒənt] Immobilienmakler
for sale [fə 'seɪl] zum Verkauf
immediately [ɪ'miːdɪətlɪ] sofort
less [les] weniger
mortgage ['mɔːgɪdʒ] Hypothek
negotiation [nɪ‚gəʊʃɪ'eɪʃən] Verhandlung
outside [aʊt'saɪd] außerhalb, vor
pay [peɪ] bezahlen
property ['prɒpətɪ] Eigentum, Anwesen
seller ['selə] Verkäufer
unless [ən'les] wenn nicht

Word group: Parts of a room

wall

ceiling ['siːlɪŋ] Decke
door [dɔː] Tür
floor [flɔː] Boden
window ['wɪndəʊ] Fenster

Word group: Furnishings

carpet – curtain – furniture – mirror

fireplace ['faɪəpleɪs] Kamin
lamp [læmp] Lampe
light [laɪt] Licht, Beleuchtungskörper
wallpaper ['wɔːl‚peɪpə] Tapete

Word group: Colours

- [ ] beige
- [ ] black
- [ ] blue
- [ ] brown
- [ ] green
- [ ] pink
- [ ] purple
- [ ] red
- [ ] white
- [ ] yellow

✏ Writing task

Imagine that you own and want to sell the house or flat that you live in now. Write a list of the things that you would tell the estate agent. Begin with:

There are (number) rooms – (number) bedrooms …
or
My flat / house is …

E-mail what you've written to someone in your class – or give it to someone to read before the next lesson starts.

Words I need

....
....
....
....
....
....

p. 94

Unit 6 (pages 43–45)

Highlight the words you'd like to learn.

ban [bæn] verbannen, ausschließen
bullring ['bʊlrɪŋ] Stierkampfarena
compete [kəm'piːt] im Wettstreit liegen, konkurrieren
earn [ɜːn] verdienen
event [ɪ'vent] Ereignis, Veranstaltung
gift shop ['gɪft ˌʃɒp] Geschenkartikelladen
grandchild ['græntʃaɪld] Enkel(kind)
hate [heɪt] hassen
hobby ['hɒbɪ] Hobby, Lieblingsbeschäftigung
I'd prefer to ... [aɪd prɪ'fɜː tə] ich würde lieber ...

I'd rather not. [aɪd 'rɑːðə nɒt] ich würde lieber nicht ...
image ['ɪmɪdʒ] Image, Bild
leisure time ['leʒə taɪm] Freizeit
let's go [ˌlets 'gəʊ] lass(t) uns gehen
mention ['menʃən] erwähnen, nennen
opinion [ə'pɪnjən] Meinung
passion ['pæʃən] Leidenschaft
politically incorrect [pə'lɪtɪklɪ ˌɪn'kərekt] politisch inkorrekt
popular ['pɒpjʊlə] beliebt, weit verbreitet
referee [ˌrefə'riː] Schiedsrichter/in
reporter [rɪ'pɔːtə] Reporter/in
skill [skɪl] Fertigkeit, Geschicklichkeit
spend (time) [spend] (Zeit) verbringen

true [truː] echt
violent ['vaɪələnt] gewalttätig, brutal

Info (page 46)

area ['eərɪə] Bereich, Gebiet
bonding ['bɒndɪŋ] Entwicklung einer Beziehung
build [bɪld] aufbauen
each other [iːtʃ 'ʌðə] einander, gegenseitig
face [feɪs] begegnen
generation [ˌdʒenə'reɪʃən] Generation
team spirit [ˌtiːm 'spɪrɪt] Teamgeist
traumatic [trɔː'mætɪk] traumatisch
trust [trʌst] vertrauen
unexpected [ˌʌnɪk'spektɪd] unerwartet

Word group: Sport

compete – referee – team

a draw [ə 'drɔː] unentschieden
goal [gəʊl] Tor
lose [luːz] verlieren
players ['pleɪəs] Spieler
point [pɔɪnt] Punkt
win [wɪn] gewinnen

Word group: Younger generations

grandchildren ['grænˌtʃɪldrən] Enkelkinder
daughter ['dɔːtə] Tochter
granddaughter ['grænˌdɔːtə] Enkeltocher
grandson ['grænsʌn] Enkelsohn
nephew ['nefjuː] Neffe
niece [niːs] Nichte
son [sʌn] Sohn

Which word goes where?

already, ever, just, never, not, yet

1 I've .... seen it. *(nie)*

2 Have you .... seen it? *(je)*

3 I've .... seen it. *(schon)*

4 I have .... seen it .... *(noch nicht)*

5 I have .... seen it. *(gerade)*

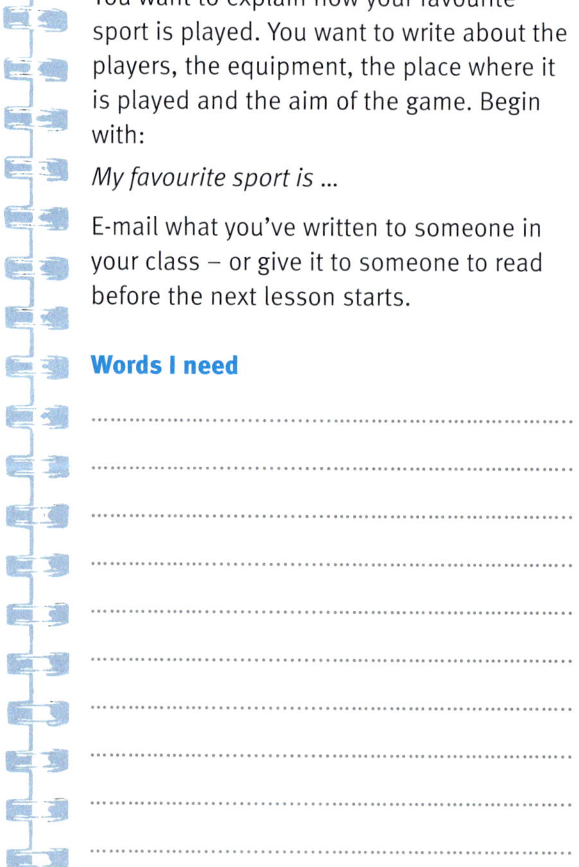

✏ Writing task

You want to explain how your favourite sport is played. You want to write about the players, the equipment, the place where it is played and the aim of the game. Begin with:

My favourite sport is ...

E-mail what you've written to someone in your class – or give it to someone to read before the next lesson starts.

Words I need

....
....
....
....
....
....
....
....
....
....
....
....

 p. 94

Unit 7 (pages 53–55)

Highlight the words you'd like to learn.

accept [əkˈsept] akzeptieren
affair [əˈfeə] Affäre, Verhältnis
afraid [əˈfreɪd] ängstlich, besorgt
angry [ˈæŋrɪ] wütend, zornig
annoyed [əˈnɔɪd] verärgert
brother [ˈbrʌðə] Bruder
busy [ˈbɪzɪ] beschäftigt
claim [kleɪm] behaupten
daughter [ˈdɔːtə] Tochter
delighted [dɪˈlaɪtɪd] erfreut
die [daɪ] sterben
disappointed [dɪsəˈpɔɪntɪd] enttäuscht
embarrassed [ɪmˈbærəst] verlegen
explode [ɪkˈspləʊd] explodieren
explosion [ɪkˈspləʊʒən] Explosion
forget [fəˈget] vergessen

furious [ˈfjʊərɪəs] wütend
get light [get ˈlaɪt] hell werden
grab [græb] greifen, grapschen
huge [hjuːdʒ] riesig
hurt [hɜːt] verletzen
injured [ˈɪndʒəd] verletzt
move in [muːv ˈɪn] einziehen
neighbour [ˈneɪbə] Nachbar
obviously [ˈɒbvɪəslɪ] offensichtlich
pour [pɔː] gießen, schütten
reason [ˈriːzn] Grund
relieved [rɪˈliːvd] erleichtert
remember [rɪˈmembə] erinnern
sad [sæd] traurig
villager [ˈvɪlɪdʒə] Dorfbewohner
wife [waɪf] Ehefrau

Info (page 56)

alarmingly [əˈlɑːmɪŋlɪ] alarmierend
anger [ˈæŋgə] Wut, Zorn

cause [kɔːz] Ursache, Grund
change [tʃeɪndʒ] (ver)ändern
crash [kræʃ] Absturz
deal (with) [ˈdiːəl (wɪð)] umgehen mit, bewältigen
deep breath [ˈdiːp ˌbreθ] tiefer Atemzug
disastrous [dɪˈzɑːstrəs] schrecklich, verheerend
(a) few [(ə) ˈfjuː] einige
imagine [ɪˈmædʒɪn] sich vorstellen
incident [ˈɪnsɪdənt] Ereignis, Zwischenfall
increase [ˌɪŋˈkriːs] ansteigen
plane [pleɪn] Flugzeug
rage [reɪdʒ] Zorn, Wut
relaxing [rɪˈlæksɪŋ] entspannend
therapy [ˈθerəpɪ] Therapie
unnecessarily [ʌnˈnesəsərəlɪ] unnötigerweise

Word group: Family members

brother – daughter – wife

Look at page 54 and at the family tree on page 86 for more family members. Write them here:

....

....

Which word goes where?

about or *by*

1 be amused .... something

2 be annoyed .... something

3 be sad .... something

4 be shocked .... something

5 be happy .... something

6 be furious .... something

7 be embarrassed .... something

8 be relieved .... something

9 be delighted .... something

10 be hurt .... someone

in or *of*

11 be disappointed .... someone

12 be afraid .... something

Write a short letter to a new friend. Begin with *Dear (name)*, and end with *Best wishes*, or *All the best*, and your name.
Write about your family beginning with:
I'd like to tell you about my family. Followed by, for example: *I've got one brother. He's married and has got two daughters. ...*

E-mail what you've written to someone in your class – or give it to someone to read before the next lesson starts.

Words I need

....

....

....

....

p. 95

Unit 8 (pages 59–61)

Highlight the words you'd like to learn.

afford [ə'fɔːd] sich leisten

artist ['ɑːtɪst] Künstler

(be) paid [(biː) 'peɪd] bezahlt werden

break-in ['breɪk ɪn] Einbruch

cheap [tʃiːp] billig

collect [kə'lekt] einsammeln, abholen

corner shop [ˌkɔːnə 'ʃɒp] Laden an der Ecke, Tante-Emma-Laden

department (of a government) [dɪ'pɑːtmənt] Ministerium

earn [ɜːn] verdienen

election [ɪ'lekʃən] Wahl

expensive [ɪk'spensɪv] teuer

explain [ɪk'spleɪn] erklären

eyebrows ['aɪbraʊz] Augenbrauen

furniture ['fɜːnɪtʃə] Möbel

government ['gʌvənmənt] Regierung

inherit [ɪn'herɪt] erben

insurance company [ɪn'ʃʊərəns ˌkʌmpənɪ] Versicherung(sgesellschaft)

invest [ɪn'vest] investieren, anlegen

lend [lend] verleihen, jdm. etwas ausleihen

light bulb ['laɪt bʌlb] Glühbirne

local ['ləʊkl] local, örtlich

look after [lʊk 'ɑːftə] betreuen, sich kümmern um

newspaper ['njuːsˌpeɪpə] Zeitung

overspend [ˌəʊvə'spend] zu viel ausgeben

pleased [pliːzd] sich freuen, zufrieden sein mit

print [prɪnt] drucken

report [rɪ'pɔːt] Bericht

rubbish bin ['rʌbɪʃ bɪn] Abfalleimer

save [seɪv] sparen

spend (money) [spend] (Geld) ausgeben

study ['stʌdɪ] Studie, Untersuchung

taxpayer ['tæksˌpeɪə] Steuerzahler

unnecessary [ʌn'nesəsərɪ] unnötig

waste [weɪst] verschwenden, vergeuden

wooden beam [ˌwʊdn 'biːm] Holzbalken

Info (page 62)

anonymous [ə'nɒnɪməs] anonym

cash [kæʃ] Bargeld

dangerous ['deɪndʒərəs] gefählich

debit card ['debɪt kɑːd] Debitkarte, Kundenkarte

feature ['fiːtʃə] ein Rolle spielen

(be) in debt [(biː) ɪn 'det] Schulden (haben)

interest ['ɪntrəst] Zins

majority [mə'dʒɒrətɪ] Mehrheit

nowadays ['naʊədeɪz] heuzutage

replace [rɪ'pleɪs] ersetzen

Word group: Parts of the body

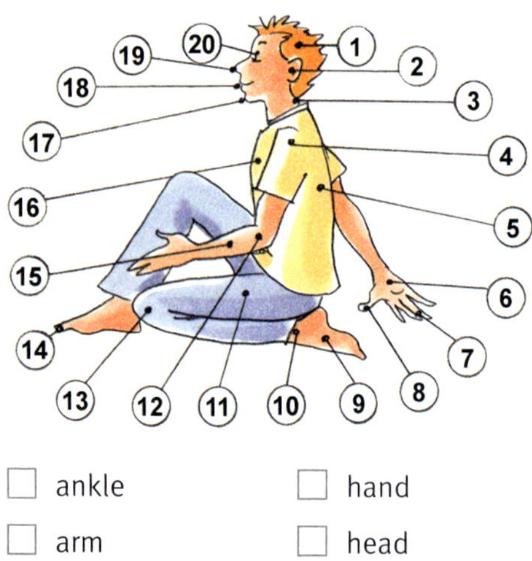

- ☐ ankle
- ☐ arm
- ☐ back
- ☐ chest
- ☐ chin
- ☐ ear
- ☐ elbow
- ☐ eye
- ☐ finger
- ☐ foot
- ☐ hand
- ☐ head
- ☐ knee
- ☐ leg
- ☐ mouth
- ☐ neck
- ☐ nose
- ☐ shoulder
- ☐ thumb
- ☐ toe

 **Writing task**

Write a short letter to your local government to complain about one of their services (see exercise 4a on page 60). Begin with:

Dear Sirs,
I feel I must complain about …

End with:

Yours faithfully,
(your name)

E-mail what you've written to someone in your class – or give it to someone to read before the next lesson starts.

Words I need

....
....
....
....
....
....

p. 95

Unit 9 (pages 65–67)

Highlight the words you'd like to learn.

add [æd] hinzufügen
bonfire ['bɒnfaɪə] Freudenfeuer
celebration [ˌseləˈbreɪʃən] Feier, Fest
close down [kləʊz 'daʊn] (sein Geschäft) schließen, zumachen
consequence ['kɒnsɪkwəns] Konsequenz, Folge, Resultat
day off [deɪ 'ɒv] arbeitsfreier Tag, Ruhetag
enclose [ɪn'kləʊz] beilegen
explode [ɪk'spləʊd] explodieren
firework ['faɪəwɜːks] Feuerwerk
fly by [ˌflaɪ 'baɪ] vergehen

full-time [ˌfʊl 'taɪm] ganztags
guild [gɪld] Gilde, Innung, Zunft
huge [hjuːdʒ] riesig
inherit [ɪnˈherɪt] erben
lifestyle ['laɪfstaɪl] Lebensstil
local ['ləʊkl] örtlich, lokal
lose [luːz] verlieren
mark [mɑːk] markieren
might [maɪt] könnte
move [muːv] umziehen
noon [nuːn] mittag
pleased [pliːzd] zufrieden, erfreut
probably ['prɒbəblɪ] vermutlich, wahrscheinlich
relative ['relətɪv] Angehöriger, Verwandter
snow [snəʊ] schneien

travel ['trævl] reisen
unfortunately [ʌnˈfɔːtʃənətlɪ] unglücklicherweise

Info (page 68)

between [bɪ'twiːn] zwischen
celebrate ['seləbreɪt] feiern
colourful [kʌləfəl] farbenfroh
each year [iːtʃ 'jɪə] jedes Jahr
earlier ['ɜːlɪə] früher
midnight ['mɪdnaɪt] Mitternacht
moon [muːn] Mond
move [muːv] bewegen, sich verändern
New Year [ˌnjuː 'jɪə] neues Jahr
throw [θrəʊ] werfen

Word group: Festivals and holidays

New Year

Write the German names of these days:

1 New Year's Day ....

2 Good Friday ....

3 Easter Sunday ....

4 Easter Monday ....

5 Christmas Eve ....

6 Christmas Day ....

7 Boxing Day ....

8 New Year's Eve ....

... and these personal celebrations:

9 anniversary ....

10 birthday ....

11 wedding ....

12 wedding anniversary ....

Word group: Days

Monday ['mandeɪ] Montag
Tuesday ['tjuːzdeɪ] Dienstag
Wednesday ['wenzdeɪ] Mittwoch
Thursday ['θɜːzdeɪ] Donnerstag
Friday ['fraɪdeɪ] Freitag
Saturday ['sætədeɪ] Samstag
Sunday ['sʌndeɪ] Sonntag

Word group: The time

6.10 = ten **past** six
6.15 = quarter **past** six
6.25 = twenty-five **past** six
6.30 = half **past** six
6.35 = twenty-five **to** seven
6.45 = quarter **to** seven
6.50 = ten **to** seven

✏ Writing task

Write about the last personal thing you celebrated and how you celebrated it. Begin with:

On (date) this (last) year I celebrated …

E-mail what you've written to someone in your class – or give it to someone to read before the next lesson starts.

Words I need

....
....
....
....
....
....

p. 95

Unit 10 (pages 71–73)

Highlight the words you'd like to learn.

alien ['eɪlɪən] Außerirdische/r
(be) allowed [(biː) ə'laʊd] erlaubt sein, dürfen
arrangement [ə'reɪndʒmənt] Vereinbarung
cause [kɔːz] verursachen
decision [dɪ'sɪʒən] Entscheidung
difference ['dɪfrəns] Unterschied
dream [driːm] Traum
earthquake ['ɜːθkweɪk] Erdbeben
(something) else [ˌ(sʌmθɪŋ) 'els] (etwas) anderes
expression [ɪk'spreʃən] Ausdruck
fear [fɪə] fürchten, Angst haben
healthy ['helθɪ] gesund
hope [həʊp] Hoffnung
include [ɪn'kluːd] enthalten
intention [ɪn'tenʃən] Absicht

look forward to [lʊk 'fɔːwəd tə] sich freuen auf
main [meɪn] hauptsächlich, Haupt-
move [muːv] umziehen
near future [ˌnɪə 'fjʊtʃə] nahe Zukunft
news bulletin [ˌnjuːz 'bʊlətɪn] Bekanntmachung
newsreader ['njuːzˌriːdə] Nachrichtensprecher/in
perform [pə'fɔːm] aufführen
publish ['pʌblɪʃ] veröffentlichen
quote [kwəʊt] zitieren
reporter [rɪ'pɔːtə] Reporter/in
retire [rɪ'taɪə] in Pension gehen
scary ['skeərɪ] furchterregend
schedule ['ʃedjuːl] Zeitplan
society [sə'saɪətɪ] Gesellschaft
suggestion [sə'dʒestʃən] Vorschlag
timetable ['taɪmˌteɪbl] Fahrplan
wish [wɪʃ] Wunsch

Info (page 74)

box [bɒks] Kasten
create [krɪ'eɪt] schaffen, schöpfen
even though [iːvən 'ðəʊ] obgleich, obwohl, wenn auch
invent [ɪn'vent] erfinden
inventor [ɪn'ventə] Erfinder/in
patent office ['peɪtənt ˌɒfɪs] Patentamt
receive [rɪ'siːv] empfangen
register ['redʒɪstə] anmelden
reject [rɪ'dʒekt] ablehnen, zurückweisen
richest ['rɪtʃɪst] reichste/r/s
recognise ['rekəgnaɪz] erkennen, wahrnehmen
success [sək'ses] Erfolg
who on earth ...? ['huː ɒn ˌɜːθ] wer in aller Welt ...?

Word group: Sources of information

Write the English words for these German word:

1 Kollegen ....

2 Freunde ....

3 Nachbarn ....

4 Zeitungen ....

5 Schwarze Bretter ....

6 Magazine ....

7 Plakate ....

8 Radio ....

9 Fernsehen ....

Which word goes where?

1 *in, into, of, on*

a) looking .... the future

b) We can meet .... Saturday.

c) a vision .... the future

d) What will happen .... the future?

2 *at, by, from, in*

a) They'll meet us .... the station.

b) a play .... Oscar Wilde

c) The aliens came .... Mars.

d) We saw them .... the restaurant.

✏ Writing task

Write about your vision of the future. What do you think people's lives will be like in ten, twenty or fifty years from now? What will society be like? Begin with:

I think that in (...) years from now everybody / people / I will ...

E-mail what you've written to someone in your class – or give it to someone to read before the next lesson starts.

Words I need

....

....

....

....

....

🔑 p. 96

Die *kursiv* gesetzten Sätze sind nicht in der Unit enthalten. Es sind zusätzliche Sätze, die Sie vielleicht lernen möchten.

Unit 1: What to say if you don't understand

- I'm sorry, could you speak more slowly, please?
- I'm sorry, I didn't understand you – could you say that again, please?
- Could you please repeat that for me?
- Sorry – I don't know what you mean.
- What does … mean?
- I only understand a little English.
- *I'm sorry – could you please explain that again?*

▶▶ Wie Sie sehen können, enthalten Sätze, die Sie verwenden können, um zu sagen, dass Sie etwas nicht verstehen, fast immer Wörter wie *sorry* oder *please*.

Unit 2: Giving advice

- Why don't you ask … ?
- I think you should ask … .
- If I were you, I'd ask … .
- It might be better to ask … .
- *Perhaps you could ask … .*

▶▶ Wörter wie *I think*, *might* und *perhaps* bewirken, dass ein Ratschlag freundlicher und nicht so sehr wie ein Befehl klingt.

Unit 2: Reacting to advice

- You must be joking!
- Yes, that's a good idea.
- Well … I need to think about it for a while.
- Yes, you may be right.
- *Thanks for the advice, I'll do that.*
- *I don't really think I should do that.*

▶▶ *You must be joking!* ist sehr informell und sollte nur verwendet werden, wenn Sie mit Freunden sprechen.

Unit 3: Likes and dislikes

- I like working in the garden.
- I don't like cleaning the windows.
- I'm not very keen on ironing.
- I hate shopping for food.
- *I can't stand cleaning the car.*
- *I dislike emptying the dishwasher.*
- *I enjoy cooking.*

▶▶ Auf die Verben *love*, *like*, *hate* folgt die *-ing*-Form. Manche Leute, vor allem Amerikaner, verwenden aber auch den Infinitiv.

Extra A: Making an appointment

- Would 10.30 suit you?
- I'm afraid 10.30 isn't possible for me.
- How about 11.30?
- Could you be here at 11.30?
- I'm afraid I can't make it in the morning.
- Would the afternoon be convenient?
- *What about 11.30?*
- *That's fine.*

▶▶ Seien Sie vorsichtig, wenn Sie von Uhrzeiten sprechen oder wenn Sie Uhrzeiten für eine Verabredung verstehen müssen. Manche Leute sagen *half past eleven* anstelle von *eleven thirty* – was *halb zwölf* auf deutsch bedeutet.

Unit 4: Inviting people

- Would you like to come to dinner?
- I'd like to invite you to dinner tomorrow.
- Why don't you come to dinner?
- I was wondering if you'd like to come to dinner tomorrow evening.

Accepting:
- Thank you very much, I'd love to come.
- That would be lovely, thank you.
- Yes, thank you, I'd be delighted.

continued …

Refusing:
- I'd love to come, but I'm afraid I can't.
- I'm really sorry, but I'm busy that evening.
- I'm sorry, I have to work on Friday.

> ▶▶ Wenn Sie auf eine Einladung oder auf ein Angebot mit *Thank you* reagieren, bedeutet das, anders als im Deutschen, dass Sie die Einladung oder das Angebot annehmen.

Unit 5: Needs and wishes

- The flat must be modern.
- If possible, there should be a balcony.
- I'd prefer to have a modern flat.
- I'd rather have an old flat than a modern one.
- I definitely need to have a double garage.
- My biggest 'must' is a garden.
- I really need to have a big flat.
- I'd love to have a view of the sea.

> ▶▶ 'd in *I'd like*, *I'd prefer*, *I'd love to* = would

Unit 6: Making and reacting to suggestions

- Shall we go to the cinema this evening?
  That's a good idea.
  Oh, I'd rather not. I'm a bit tired today.
- Let's go to the cinema this evening.
  Oh yes, let's.
- Why don't we go to the cinema tomorrow?
  Well actually, I'd prefer to stay at home.
- *How about going to the cinema tomorrow.
  Sorry, I can't. I'm working tomorrow. What about next week?*

> ▶▶ Wenn Sie ablehnend auf einen Vorschlag reagieren, sollten Sie eine kurze Erklärung geben.

Extra B: On the phone

- Hold on, please.
- I'm sorry, the line's busy / engaged.
- The line's free now.
- I'll put you through.
- *I'm sorry, he isn't here at the moment.*
- *Can I take a message?*
- *Could you call back later?*
- *I'll ask him to call you back.*
- *Could you ask him to call me back, please.*

> ▶▶ Wenn Sie z.B. eine Firma anrufen, wird normalerweise der Name der Firma genannt. Wenn Sie jemanden privat anrufen, meldet sich der Teilnehmer mit *Hello* oder nennt die Telefonnummer. Telefonnummern werden als Einzelziffern gesprochen: *372605 = three seven two six oh five*. Etwas anders ist es, wenn in der Nummer eine Ziffer doppelt vorkommt: *459906 = four five double nine oh six*.

Unit 7: Talking about feelings

- I am delighted.
- I was very happy about it.
- I feel a bit annoyed about it.
- I felt very relieved.
- *I've never felt so sad in all my life.*

> ▶▶ Im Zusammenhang mit Wörtern, die Gefühle beschreiben, verwendet man häufig Wörter wie *very* und *a bit*, um die Tiefe des Gefühl genau zu treffen.

Unit 8: Obligation and ability

- I **have to** work on Sunday. = Ich muss …
- I **don't have to** work tomorrow. = Ich muss nicht …
- I **must** phone my mother. = Ich muss …
- I **mustn't** forget to call her. = Ich darf nicht …
- I **can** see my friends tomorrow. = Ich kann …
- I **can't** go away for the weekend. = Ich kann nicht …

> ▶▶ Achten Sie auf den Bedeutungsunterschied zwischen dem Englischen *I mustn't* und dem Deutschen *Ich muss nicht*.

Unit 9: Probability and possibility

- I **will be** there. (100% certain that I'll be there)
- I'll **probably** be there. (90% certain that I'll be there)
- I **might** be there. (50% certain that I'll be there)
- I **probably won't** be there. (90% certain that I won't be there)
- I **won't** be there. (100% certain that I won't be there)

⏩ Die 50%ige Wahrscheinlichkeit *(might)* kann auch ausgedrückt werden durch: *I may be there* oder *Perhaps I'll be there.*

Unit 10: Wishes, hopes and dreams

- I'd love to do that.
- I hope I'll be able to do that.
- My dream future would be to do that.
- All I want is to do that.
- *My aim is to do that.*

⏩ Das Verb *wish* wird nicht verwendet, um über die Zukunft zu sprechen, das Nomen *wish* jedoch kann verwendet werden, um über die Zukunft zu sprechen, wie z.B.: *My greatest wish is to do that.*

Complaining

- *I'm sorry, but I have a complaint to make.*
- *Excuse me, I'd like to complain about …*
- *I'm sorry to have to complain, but …*
- *I really must complain about …*

⏩ Briten sind oft ein bisschen zu höflich, wenn sie sich beschweren – sehr oft beginnen sie ihren Satz mit *I'm sorry* oder *Excuse me … .*

Dealing with complaints

- *Thank you for telling me about this, I'll …*
- *I'm very sorry, can I do anything to help?*
- *I'm so sorry for the inconvenience.*
- *I'm afraid I can't help you.*

⏩ Menschen, die im Dienstleistungsbereich arbeiten, wird geraten, Beschwerden ernst zu nehmen und sofort zu akzeptieren.

Apologising and reacting to apologies

- *I'm sorry (about that).*
- *Oh that's all right.*
- *It doesn't matter.*
- *No problem.*

⏩ Es ist wichtig, eine echte Entschuldigung (zumindest für nicht so schwerwiegende Dinge) freundlich zu akzeptieren.

Asking for and granting permission

- *May I open the window?*
- *Yes, of course.*
- *Actually, I'd rather you didn't.*
- *Do you mind if I open the window?*
- *No, of course not.*

⏩ Die letzte Reaktion oben *No, of course not* bedeutet, dass es in Ordnung ist, das Fenster zu öffnen: *No, of course I don't mind if you open the window.*

Introducing oneself and others

I'm … / My name's …
I'd like to introduce you to …
Can I introduce you to …
This is …
Pleased to meet you.
Nice to meet you.
How do you do?

⏩ *How do you do?* wird hauptsächlich in formellen privaten und geschäftlichen Situationen verwendet.

Eating and drinking

Eating: Bon Appetit! / Enjoy your meal.
Drinking: To your health. / Cheers.

⏩ Briten sagen oft überhaupt nichts, wenn sie mit dem Essen beginnen. *Bon Appetit* ist formeller als *Enjoy your meal*, und *To your health* ist formeller als *Cheers.*

Your personal notes: